D1248959

THE STORY OF INDIA

by the same author

RIVER BOY OF KASHMIR

STAR OF INDIA

EMPTY TOWER

LITTLE FLUTE PLAYER

(*published by William Morrow and Company*)

LITTLE BOAT BOY

THE THIRTEENTH STONE

PETER HOLT, P.K.

SWORD OF A WARRIOR

(*published by Harcourt, Brace and Company*)

THE STORY OF

Illustrated with drawings by Jeanyee Wong, and with photographs

JEAN BOTHWELL

INDIA

HARCOURT, BRACE AND COMPANY
NEW YORK

FIRST EDITION

LIBRARY OF CONGRESS CATALOG CARD NUMBER: 52-10062

PRINTED IN THE UNITED STATES OF AMERICA

FOR MY GOD-CHILD JEAN INGRID SANDALL

CONTENTS

ILLUSTRATIONS

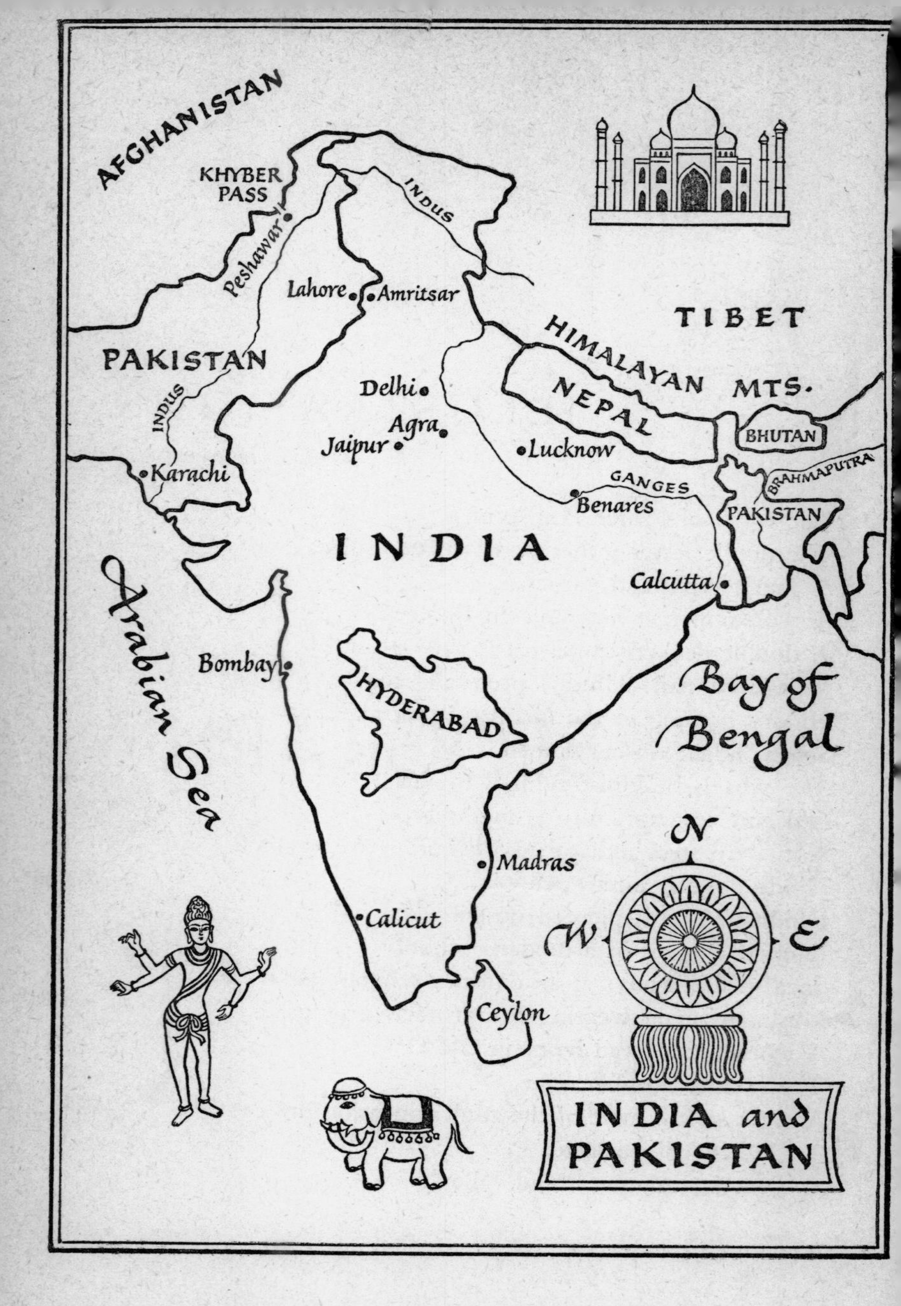
AFGHANISTAN
KHYBER PASS
Peshawar
INDUS
Lahore
Amritsar
TIBET
HIMALAYAN MTS.
PAKISTAN
NEPAL
Delhi
INDUS
Agra
Jaipur
Lucknow
BHUTAN
BRAHMAPUTRA
Karachi
GANGES
Benares
PAKISTAN
INDIA
Calcutta
Arabian Sea
Bombay
HYDERABAD
Bay of Bengal
N
Madras
W
E
Calicut
Ceylon
INDIA and PAKISTAN

I. GEOGRAPHY

INDIA is a beautiful land. It has tall mountains, swift rivers, strange trees and fruits, and dense tropical forests, full of wild animals. It has many customs which seem odd to Westerners, but they help to distinguish India from any other country of the world.

India was the first country to grow cotton. Most of the pepper used by world markets is grown in India. Curry, a mixture of spices, now becoming very popular in American restaurants, is an Indian way of seasoning food.

The geography of any land, the things that land produces, and the climate, have a strong effect on the life of the people, and through them, on its history. This is especially true of India. This great subcontinent lies in two zones of climate, the temperate and the torrid. The weather in the North gives the people there three sharply defined seasons in the year. They are: the mild cold, the extremely dry, and the very wet. South India enjoys a more even temperature the year round, which assures more comfortable living. This condition of weather alone has caused a great difference between the customs, the living habits, and the development of Indian people in North and South.

But all of the things which set India apart from any other country, when understood together, make that land an exciting place on the map of the world.

1

INDIA ON THE MAP

WHEN ONE first looks at the map, India appears to be a giant triangle, upside down, with its point thrusting into the Indian Ocean. Along the base of the triangle are high mountain ranges, separating it from Central Asia. These are the Himalayas and the Karakoram, the Hindu Kush, the Pamirs and the Pir Panjal chain. They stretch for sixteen hundred miles across the northern border but they do not completely shut India in, away from her neighbors. There are passes through them on the northeast and northwest, along high valleys, which have been used for hundreds of years by caravans going back and forth between India and Iran, Turkestan, Tibet and China for trade, by pioneers seeking new homes and by soldiers for conquest.

Though seeming to be a peninsula on the map, India is really a subcontinent. It is divided by the Vindhya range of mountains in the central part, almost directly across the middle, into a natural North and South. These two regions, even today, are distinctly different in culture, speech and traditions. The climate and appearance of the land on either side of these mountains, in North and South, have their distinct differences as well.

Because of its many rivers India is a garden land, with only a small area, comparatively, that is desert. But the word garden has a meaning there somewhat different from our western word. If a caller is told that an Indian gentleman is not in his house, that he has gone to his garden, and the caller has business urgent enough to follow him there, he does not step out into a yard a few feet from a house door. He may go out into the country a mile or so, or make a shorter trip to the outskirts of the town. Upon arriving at the *bagh* (garden) he is quite likely to discover that it is a grove of mango trees through which are clay paths swept clean, and that in the center is a well with a small pavilion nearby to rest in when the day is warm.

A caretaker keeps the mango grove neat and on occasion the whole family goes out to the garden for some special celebration, a birthday or a religious holiday. When the fruit is ripe the caretaker is useful to protect it from thieves. Produce merchants often buy a whole crop before it is picked and provide their own watchmen to look after the purchase. But no one can do much about the parrots. Wild ones, in great flocks, swoop down on a garden in a bright flash of shining green wings. They like mangoes, too.

Many of the large cities of the north have Horticultural Gardens which are really parks; sometimes there is a zoo in connection. All of such government gardens have magnificent flower beds.

The hill slopes of the lower Himalayas are terraced, and small irregular-sized pocket handkerchief fields are edged with stone to keep the dirt from washing away. The hill people grow rice in this fashion and other grains, and apple trees flourish in protected valleys. The slanting fields look like an odd checkerboard of many shades of green and yellow.

Away to the north in Kashmir are the famous gardens of the old Moghul kings who invaded India in the early part of the sixteenth century and united a great deal of the country under one rule for a while. They liked the sound of running water among their trees and flowers. Little channels leading from a central well or fountain or stream divide grass plots and flower beds into geometrical patterns of lovely color. Shade trees, usually the *chenar*, like our sycamore in the United States, give cool protection from the sun. There is peace among the trees of an Indian garden. The old kings liked to smoke there and entertain their friends.

A garden can also mean, for India's many poor people, a single plant of marigold in a flowerpot beside a low doorway. Or, in a town, where a merchant houses his family in the particular bazaar in which he does business, their garden is a courtyard behind the shop. It may have grass, but it is usually a space of hard-tamped earth with large foliage plants called *crotons* growing in enormous pottery jars, edging the paths and the porches which lead to the courtyard.

Rivers in any land provide more than a means of travel or water for crops and gardens. In India, from long association with religious beliefs, rivers have a sacred significance and of them all, the Ganges is probably the most famous. It flows across India for fifteen hundred miles, providing irrigation water in some places in the plains and electric power in others before it merges with the ocean in the Bay of Bengal. Hindus believe firmly that bathing in its sacred waters will cure them of disease and wash away their sins and that to die on its banks or to have the ashes of their burned bodies spread on its surface will take the spirit immediately to heaven.

So, they bathe in it in thousands, particularly at Benares, a city of pilgrimage, and they drink its water and commit to it the ashes of their dead. Their belief in the power of this mighty stream is supported by a scientific fact. Experts in sanitation have examined and analyzed its water and it has been proved that germs do not stay alive in it for more than twenty-four hours. By some mysterious force the water of this one river in all of India has a purifying property which protects its worshippers. Here geography and religion link with science.

One of the rivers of India has given the land its English name. The Greek word for *river* is *indos*. When Alexander the Great brought his army of Greeks to the Northwest border of India in 327 B.C. they made a proper name of the word and applied it to one river, known today as the Indus. The word *India* is only a modification of that name.

Religion is much more a part of intimate daily life in India than anywhere else on earth. It is even a part of the geography, when the rivers are sacred and the great range of northern mountains, the Himalayas, is believed to be the home of the gods.

South India is high table land above a coastal plain on the east and west. Its climate is more even, and it has a tropical beauty in garden and hill and river that is lacking in the north.

But rivers and gardens and mountains, however sacred or lovely or remarkable are, after all, only parts of a map. It is people who make a map important, by the changes which their action or inaction bring about in it.

2

TRAVEL AND COMMUNICATION

SINCE TIME BEGAN, man has built roads upon which he could move about. Throughout history there have been many famous roadways. Among these, in India, there was the Royal Road made in the time of King Asoka who reigned from 272 to 231 B.C. It was twelve hundred miles long, leading from Taxila on the northern frontier to modern Patna, in Orissa. There were wells and trees and rest places for travelers on this wide thoroughfare, and special officials appointed by King Asoka were charged with the responsibility of its upkeep.

Equally well known was the Grand Trunk Road, which was old when Kipling's Kim and his lama walked that way toward Benares, the holy city of the Hindus, on the lama's search for the River of Rama's Bow. It is still in use, from Peshawar in the north (now in Pakistan) to Calcutta on the Hooghly River, a wide way across India where single bullock carts squeak along unhurriedly and motor cars leave them far behind in a thick cloud of dust.

It takes time to travel any road and there was much need for haste in early days when danger threatened. Fire could be seen from far off and so watch towers were built at intervals along highways. If an enemy were seen approaching at night, a beacon could be lighted and a message sent to the man in the next tower, miles away. Sunlight and a piece of mirror were used in the daytime to send news.

The modern roads of India, which are bringing the people closer together by means of the motor bus and lorry than bullock and camel carts have ever done, have followed the original foundations of ancient Moghul highways.

Those old Moghul planners were shrewd. Along a good road, news from the farthest edges of their States could come faster than along a poor one. They originated a system of communication which is followed in modern form even today in remote parts of India where no vehicle can go easily. A band of runners carried messages and official despatches in relays of three or four miles each. As had been done in King Asoka's time there were rest houses and police stations along the way and shade trees gave protection from the blazing sun. If there was no village at the point of the three-mile halt, sentry boxes were set up, where the fresh runner could wait for the one coming.

Each of these men carried a whip about three feet long, "two cubits" the old record reads, with small bells fastened at the end. The jingle of the bells could be heard far down the trail, and warned the next runner that the expected one would shortly appear. It is recorded that a message could be carried two hundred miles in twenty-four hours in this fashion. Modern relay races are done in the same way, each runner touching the next one at the end of his own lap.

After the Moghuls had departed and before the building of extensive railways in India during the Empire period (1858 to 1947), the only means of sending the mails inland from the coast was by bullock cart or the swifter *tonga*. The latter were heavier than the same sort of vehicle used in towns, and because of the longer journeys and greater loads it was necessary to have two horses, instead of one. Travelers reached the interior by this means, paying a fee for the privilege. It was unsafe to journey at night, particularly through the jungle, because of wild animals and robbers. For this reason rest houses were established for the mail carriers and their passengers across the great India plains.

The word for mail is *dak*. The carrier vehicle became the *dak ghari* (mail carriage) and the rest hous was known as a *dak bungalow*. Each place had its own staff and they provided food and other services for both travelers and beasts.

The bungalows were picturesque, built in the style of the country, one-storied, with whitewashed plaster walls inside and out, and thatched, peaked roofs. Across the front and sometimes at one end a deep veranda connected the rooms and provided an outdoor lounging place. The furniture was generally heavy, made of teakwood. The crockery dishes were thick and white, and the stone floors were covered with *coir* matting and cotton rugs. Each traveler brought his own bedding. Some of these houses are still in use, serving as hotels when government officials inspect district offices.

With the coming of the railroads the need for the tonga and the crosscountry method of carrying the mails ended, but the foot couriers were retained to carry letters and papers to far-off places in the hills and the Indian jungle.

Summer visitors in the Kumaon, a lower range of the Himalayas, may often see the dak runners lounging about the post office in the big hill stations, waiting for their loads. Sometimes they may meet them jogging along a lonely path. Their gait is neither walk nor run yet it covers the distance swiftly.

They are sturdy little brown hill men, with muscular bare legs, well worn clothing, and a tight-fitting skull cap on the head. Coarse, very black hair shows round the edges and their eyes, much wrinkled at the corners, are sharp as an eagle's. They, too, carry bells which sound like those used on an American sleigh, but theirs are mounted on a wood staff, instead of a whip. The relay warning is no longer necessary. But hill roads wind in many hairpin curves and the bells are a protection against accident round the next bend. A string of burros burdened with fat bags of charcoal might take up the whole width of the path. The bells are also a sign to all on the road that the runner is on official business and it is against the law to delay him.

The letter writer is a familiar figure in most Indian bazaars, or sitting cross-legged on the veranda of the post office with his bottle of ink and pens ready on his low desk. For a small fee he will receive the dictation of a countryman who wishes to send a message to a member of his family or to conclude some business deal, which he is unable to write for himself. There is always a little haggling before they start. That is the Indian way. They enjoy it. So much for the stamp or the post card and so much for the job. That the business of the person dictating becomes the common news of the bazaar does not stop him. He has no choice if his message is urgent.

The history of the Indian Postal Service provides much interesting information for American stamp collectors. General mail service for the public was not begun until 1837, while the British East India Company was still governing India. A rate of two annas (about four cents) per letter for every one hundred miles of travel was charged in the beginning and this made necessary the coining of "copper tickets to the value of two annas," so the old record reads. The copper pieces were exchanged for the privilege of sending the letter and to this day school children and office boys call postage stamps "tickets". Paper stamps were not issued for general use until 1854 when the postal rate was much reduced. The stamps were unperforated and not gummed and they bore the likeness of Queen Victoria. In 1900 the International Postal Union decided that member nations all over the world should use the same color for corresponding denominational values in stamps. This caused some changes in the coloring of India postage and the new issue was the last one to show the profile of Victoria, the first Queen-Empress of India.

The honor of carrying mail by air for the first time in the world is claimed by India. On February 19, 1911, 6,500 pieces of first class mail were flown by a French aviator a short distance between two points in United Provinces, now known as Uttar Pradesh. In 1929 India issued a special set of air-mail stamps, the first country in the British Commonwealth to do so.

In 1931 New Delhi was officially designated as the capital of India, settling a long argument as to whether or not it should remain in Calcutta. To honor the new capital six denominations of postage stamps were issued, showing buildings in old and New Delhi, with the head of King George V inset at the right.

Four years later, on the occasion of King George V's Silver Jubilee, a set of seven stamps, similarly designed, showing buildings elsewhere in India, was issued.

In 1937 a much larger issue, ten stamps in all, was brought out to show the various methods of transport of the mails. The old tonga carrier appears on one and a dak runner on another. George VI had become King and it was his profile which appeared in the medallion at the right of each of these new stamps.

At the close of World War II another set of stamps of commemorative size was issued to celebrate the victory. The design was the same for each denomination, the King's medallion and a Sword of Victory spanning the globe.

Following India's independence a "Jai Hind" (meaning Victory to India) set of three stamps came out, showing the new State Seal, the new flag, and an airplane in flight. A supply was flown to the United States to meet the demands of collectors, another first in India's postal history.

All of the commemorative issues are beautifully made and colored and are a fine addition to any collection.

A sheet of India postage stamps was the beginning of the valuable and famous collection of old and rare stamps made by King George V. It was during a State visit to India when he was Prince of Wales that he saw the stamps and purchased the sheet.

The spoken language of India has given some words

to our modern English vocabulary. *Loot* comes from the Urdu (North India) verb *lutna*, meaning to steal. *Thug*, our word for a vicious thief, comes from the name of the thief caste, the *thagas*, who live by robbing and killing. The derivation of our word *rice* has followed a devious route. The old Romans obtained rice from the province of Orissa, and named it in Latin *oryza sativa*. Another source is the Tamil (South India) for the word itself, *arisi*. However it came, *rice* was a gift to us from India.

Chapattie language was an old and secret means of getting word about the country when speech was dangerous unless the real message was carefully disguised. A chapattie is a piece of unleavened bread, baked over hot coals, flat and round like an American pancake. One or two of them, handled significantly, or divided into the right number of pieces, could indicate a date when some event was to take place, but such a message could have meaning only for the person expecting it. Runners between villages in a sort of relay race could get word over a wide district in a single night. This system was used effectively by the plotters who persuaded Indian troops to rise against their English officers at the time of the famous mutiny in 1857.

There is also the language of the lotus flower, sacred in Buddhism, with a hidden significance which has been closely guarded for years by those who know. This, too, was used in those troubled days of '57.

More romantic and mysterious in India than in perhaps any other country of the world, unless it be Africa, and linked with the chapattie and the lotus, is the primitive "grapevine" means of spreading news. To the American who is a newcomer to Indian living and ways of doing things it is often more annoying than amusing. Indians are clever at interpreting the meaning of a tone or a look and are often ninety-five percent accurate, even when they do not understand English. Because of this, gossip in the bazaars sometimes has the quality of mind reading. This ability of the Indian has been put to good use in the Intelligence service of the Army.

For educated people there are newspapers and magazines to read, giving the most up-to-date opinions on all that is going on in the world. These are printed in Hindi, the official language of the government, and in other scripts, as well as English. Several publishing houses, North and South, and in the port cities, turn out a fine lot of books every year. The number of Indian writers is increasing with the presentation of journalism courses in the higher schools.

But 85% of India's population is illiterate, that is, they cannot read or write. This is a handicap to any nation, and systematic adult education is going on in some of the villages. It is operated somewhat on the plan of the pebble and the pool. One man in a village is taught to write his name and to read simple printing. He is pledged to teach another man what he himself has learned. The women are doing it, too. It is a little like measles or chickenpox. It is "catching".

For local travel, everybody who can get hold of a bicycle rides one now in India, even out in the country. Anything on two wheels that can be made to run, is used. A "wheel" is especially popular with students and missionaries. Bicycles with rickshaws attached are gradually replacing tongas in some of the larger cities of the North. The tonga for city use is a light, two-wheeled cart, drawn by one horse, in which driver and fare sit back to back. There is a canopy overhead, on a framework, which can be folded and pulled down like the top of a convertible motor car.

Camel carts are two-decked affairs with a cloth canopy, and latticed sides. They are still in use in Rajputana and in some parts of Uttar Pradesh. They are odd-looking carriages but they accommodate a whole family and its goods. Camels' odor and disposition in India are no better than they are in Africa or in an American circus.

There used to be closed carriages looking like narrow, oblong boxes on wheels, with little doors on the sides which could be rolled shut. These were called *band gharies*, *band* meaning *closed* and *ghari*, carriage. These were horse drawn also, and the driver perched high in front, on the outside.

As everywhere else in the world, the price of even a horse's food is rising and this will probably mean the passing of many picturesque if uncomfortable conveyances.

In the hills there is still the slow, sure-footed pony, if one cares to ride that way up from the end of the railway. Or, for choice, there is the *dandy*.

This is a sort of carrying chair made of wood, shaped a little like a canoe with a seat in one end. The points are suspended by heavy leather straps from stout poles which four coolies fit to their shoulders and so swing the passenger up the winding roads.

These coolies are usually hill farmers who leave their fields to the women in the summer holiday season, to make some extra cash for the family. They are a friendly, cheerful people. From constant climbing they are slender and muscular and seem not to mind heavy loads. Sometimes a fifth coolie trails along, carrying some of the traveler's hand luggage and he spells the others at intervals at the poles.

It is customary to arrange for the price of the trip at the start and all know that at the end a little extra should be paid as good measure for a safe journey. If the passenger is generous the men go away grinning, their white teeth gleaming against their dark, smooth-shaven faces.

In South India, along the quiet water ways of Travancore, a boat called a *vallom* takes the place of tonga and bullock cart of the North. The vallom carries a great deal of the freight traffic of the south country as well as passengers. It is a long, narrow, roomy craft, with woven mat roof, fastened to a framework. The middle mat over the widest part of the boat can be removed, allowing for loading, and put in place again when ready for the journey, unless the passengers want to see out. A boatman with a pole stands on a little platform, forward, to steer.

Travel on an Indian railway train is a wonderful experience. There is so much to see at every station along the way that one is never bored. The carriages open at the side, directly onto the platform, though in recent years, both North and South, corridor trains have been introduced. There are separate carriages for the women and at every stop their menfolk get out and go along the platform to see if the family is all right.

Their talking adds to the deafening noise at any train halt. Sweetmeat sellers and fruit and tea vendors walk along the platform below the carriage windows, shouting their wares. There are carriers of "water for Hindus" and uniformed attendants from the dining car, hurrying along with trays of meals that have been ordered by passengers in carriages. Coolies struggle along with loads of luggage on their heads and backs, trying to find the reserved seats of their patrons. Fights occur. A policeman lounges along, trying not to see too much. There isn't time enough to get at the cause of any fight before the train starts.

One wonders why so many people are traveling. It is hard on the babies. They cry. Perhaps there is a religious festival somewhere down the line. Perhaps that family in the next carriage is going to a wedding in a former home town. It sounds that way, from scraps of talk that drift in.

The guard whistles and carriage doors bang shut. The engine jerks, backs the train a little, then gathers it together in a mighty leap forward and away it goes, to repeat the whole thing at the next stop where there will be more vendors, more new passengers and the usual noise. Indian travel is fun.

3

PLANTS AND SEASONS

INDIA LIES in two zones, the temperate and the torrid. Though all of the great triangle lies above or north of the equator, the southern half enjoys a fairly even climate the year round, while in the north, on the wide plains of India, they have a three-seasonal year. It is divided into a short, mild "cold weather", from the end of October to the first part of February; a short, extremely dry season known as the "hot weather", lasting from the end of February to late June; then the monsoon wind begins to blow and it rains practically every day until late September, with a steaming-off period in early October. This kind of variety cannot help but have its effect on the people and on their way of living.

The monsoon, a seasonal wind, is India's life line. Blowing from the southwest at the end of June, across the Indian Ocean and the Bay of Bengal on the east, it meets with the cooler air from the Himalayas. The rain thus caused falls back on the Indian plain, on Bengal's jungles and the plateaus of the south. It soaks the land thoroughly, providing moisture for a whole growing season in the later "cold weather".

Because of the seasonal rains an umbrella became a symbol of importance in India. It is even seen in the decorataion of Indian buildings. In the detailed laws of the Hindu caste it is written that some of the people may not carry one. An ancient king, Harsha, one of the successors of King Asoka, had a great desire to unite the country—to bring all of India "under one umbrella." In Lucknow, in the old days, a service Club got its name—the *Chhattar Manzil*—from the stone umbrellas on its roof. The building is now used for government offices. That is appropriate inasmuch as India is now at last all brought together under one government umbrella.

The coming of the monsoon is watched for anxiously by many people. If there is a heavy rainfall the farmer knows he will have good crops and he will be able to raise enough grain to feed his family during the coming year, as well as to pay his share to the landlord. The merchant watches for it because the rate of the rainfall affects prices in the bazaar. If there is a poor rainfall and the rice and wheat left from the preceding year are not enough to feed all the peopie, then there will be a famine. Several times in India's long history there have been periods of severe food shortage when thousands of people have died because they couldn't get enough to eat. Distribution has been partly to blame. Greed for profit has entered in. But the rain is the great factor, kind one year and cruel another.

The earth soaks up the rain during the steamy weeks of July and August and September. In the part of the country where rice grows, work can go on in the paddy fields even during the rainy season. Other cultivators must wait until the end of the rains to put in their seeds and plants.

Toward the end of September, there is one last roar and crash and rumble from the skies and the monsoon season ends in a great flourish of a downpour. If seeds have been put in too soon, they are sometimes washed out and all the planting has to be done again. But when the rains are really over, the earth steams in the sun, the birds come out of their hiding places and flash across the gardens looking for insects. The crested hoopoe struts along, ruffling his tawny feathers. Then he goes after his food with his long pointed bill. Crows caw happily or meanly, whatever their mood, from every tree. In the evergreens the wood doves add their mournful, gentle note to the harsher sounds of other birds.

The whole countryside is glad the rains are ended for another year. The crows fly down to follow the ploughman, looking for a meal of grubs. The sweet smell of new-turned earth is everywhere. It is a lovely season in North India. The days are warm for a little longer, and all the doors and windows stand open, in town and country alike. At night, as October wanes and November comes in, a fire on the hearth is welcome. It is an odd fact that this chilly time is North India's best growing season.

There are no fences, no windmills, no big barns with hay mows in the Indian landscape. A field will sometimes have a cactus hedge to separate it from a road when there are no trees for that purpose, but there is nothing like a New England stone fence or a trim wooden or barbed wire one, following section lines, such as we see in the Middle West of our own country. Roads link some of the villages and there are more tiny places which are far distant from highways. Occasionally water reflects the blue of the sky, where a canal cuts across the land from the Ganges or the Jumna River, carrying water to the fields so that the good work begun in the earth by the monsoon rains may go on.

A tree planting week has been established in India in an effort to prevent soil erosion on river banks and other places. A scientific plan for this has been prepared which will give general benefit to men and animals. Throughout all of India, trees will be selected to grow in friendly soil and in the proper climate. Thus, one of the natural beauties of India will be preserved by sensible and careful planting. The regard of Indians for trees is not new. In the writings of the ancient wise ones it is recorded that one tree is worth ten sons.

Not all of the trees of India shed their leaves at the same time, so that here and there in the landscape there will be a brown, dead-looking stick of a thing, when every other is in full leaf. But later, when all its neighbors are stark and dry, that lone tree will put out its fresh garment of green and observe its own cycle of the seasons.

The mango tree, along with the fir and arbor vitae and evergreen, never drops its leaves. That is, there is never a time when it is leafless. New ones push the old ones off and its greatest seasonal change is the blooming of small, pale, oddly fragrant clusters of flowers which are washed off the tree in drifts in the first rains.

The great northern plains have a different beauty in the dry season, for then some of the most gorgeous of the flowering trees are in bloom. When all the plant world seems to have dried up with the increasing warmth then the tulip or silk-cotton tree puts out clusters of scarlet blossoms on a bare branch. The ripe pods which follow are full of a floss like our milkweed, and this makes wonderful stuffing for cushions.

Another tree with a scarlet flower is the *gul mohur* and its name is taken from that of an ancient gold coin of Persia which was worth about five dollars in American money. The flowers come before the leaves, which are fine and feathery like those on our locust trees.

There is an old road in the province of Uttar Pradesh, connecting two large towns, which was long ago planted with *kuchnar* trees at intervals on either side. This tree blooms in March or early April. Its blossoms are a rosy-lavender and white, something like a small orchid with one petal deeper in color than the rest. That roadside is like a garden, set in the middle of fields.

The *amaltas*, the Indian laburnum, is sometimes called the "golden rain tree" because of its blossoms which hang like long yellow tassels among the pale green leaves. This tree has been planted along several of the streets in New Delhi, the capital, because of its great decorative quality. It grows very tall and has a ragged kind of beauty when the long yellow tassels have turned into brown seed pods.

The *banyan* tree, which sends roots out into the air from its branches to grow until they reach the earth and form another tree trunk, is known the world over. The famous one in the Indian Botanical Garden in Calcutta, though the main trunk was cut down in 1925, now covers a space of one thousand feet in circumference and reaches to a height of eighty-eight feet. On one of King Asoka's pillars remaining from ancient times there is an inscription which affirms that he caused banyan trees to be planted "for shade to cattle and men".

Many of India's trees are sacred or have some medicinal quality in bark or leaf. It was under a *pipal* (peepul) tree, the green bo tree of Gaya, that the Lord Buddha received enlightenment. When Hinduism claimed him as one of its own, that tree became sacred. It has a white, smooth bark, not unlike our American birch. But it is a larger, sturdier tree than our lady-of-the-forest. The pipal has no blossom, but the dark glossy green leaves are beautifully shaped, something like a heart. A way has been found to soak off the green covering and when the leaf is dried, a fine white lacy skeleton remains which makes a nice bookmark. By walking along an Indian roadside one may see how this tree is regarded. A small rude shrine is usually to be found beneath it, with offerings to the spirit of the tree.

The *nim*, pronounced *neem*, tree has small, insignificant greenish-white blossoms, growing in clusters, which produce small nutlike fleshy pods. An oil is pressed from these, and some of the solid matter which is left, when mixed at the roots of poinsettias, will kill the white ants which eat and destroy this flower. Dried nim leaves laid in layers between winter blankets will keep moths out.

In April the rhododendron blooms in the Himalayas and wild orchids grow abundantly on the lower slopes. There are also wild, single dahlias. Ferns sprout from the moss which clings to the trees, and Jack-in-the-pulpit grows rankly.

Rudyard Kipling made the *deodar* famous in his tales of the Simla hills. It is a graceful tree of the evergreen family and lines many a familiar hill path and avenue leading to government houses and churchyards.

Teakwood, the Indian mahogany, in stained or natural color, is used extensively for fine made-to-order cabinet work. Teak trees give every Indian gardener a great problem. Their giant leaves dry and fall during the cold weather. Small boys earn pocket money clearing the flower beds of these unsightly cast-offs.

The *arica* tree produces the nut which is combined with the *betel* leaf to make *pan*, the mixture which is chewed everywhere in India.

The dry, wrinkled, reddish-brown nut from the soap berry tree, called *ritha*, is used by women and girls for washing their hair. The nuts are boiled for the purpose and the soapy liquid makes a perfect shampoo.

At Christmas time, gardens on the plains are at their best. Poinsettias bloom in gigantic bush clusters higher than a tall person. Tiny white butterflies appear and flutter in clouds above their golden hearts all day, in and out, tirelessly. No other plant in the garden receives such attention. The butterflies disappear when the poinsettias return to their all-green state.

The colors on an Indian fruit stall, arranged in a slanting series of shelves, are as gay as the peoples' clothing. There are small yellow bananas, scarcely four inches long, called plantains. In May, in Lucknow, there are little white-fruited melons called *safedas*, because *safed* is the word for *white*. Apples come down from the Kulu Valley in the Himalayas. Loose-skinned oranges, like the American tangerine, but a great deal larger, are shipped to port cities and North and South in the cold weather, from Nagpur in Central India. There are always piles of dates from Arabia. Also there are a number of fruits of the country which are not known elsewhere. The *bher*, a sort of plum and very tart, is one of these.

The season of the late rains is the time for mangoes. They crowd the market then, in all sizes and shades from blush red to pale green, full of deep golden fruit clinging to a single fibre-matted seed. There is a faint suggestion of turpentine in the flavor which is not unpleasant after one has acquired a taste for this fruit. In the search by scientists for every possible use of India's food resources, a way has been found to make flour from the heart of mango seeds to be used by people and animals alike. It has a high caloric content.

Guavas take the place of mangoes in the cold weather. This is a smaller fruit, shaped something like a lemon. It gives off an extremely pungent odor if kept in a closed room. When stewed, the pale yellow flesh turns pink, and from it a rich, clear crimson jelly is made, highly valued as a delicacy in American markets.

Papaya, or *papita*, rich in pepsin, a golden-hearted fruit like a melon, but borne on a tree, comes in the summer months. This fruit is produced from a father and a mother tree, that strange phenomenon of the plant world.

Though trees are one of India's greatest treasures,

fields and gardens yield enormous commercial crops of various sorts. When the mustard, golden with flowers in January, has ripened, oil is pressed out of the seeds and sold for cooking. It has a good flavor and makes mild food taste better. It is also very nourishing.

Cotton-growing in India is in process of change from short staple to the long staple variety which is now in greater demand as it makes finer cloth. There is a great future ahead in cotton when India develops the sort of machinery needed to compete with the cotton cloth markets of the world.

Pepper grows on a vine in Malabar, along the southwestern coast of India. Both black and white pepper come from the same vine. The fruit is a small berry, which we know, when it is dried, as a peppercorn. When it is ground, the outer husk of the berry is the black pepper we use on American tables and in our kitchens. The white pepper is the inner part.

The pepper industry provides work for many people. The harvest from all the small plantations around is taken to the city of Cochin for sifting and sorting and packing. A six-hundred-pound weight of pepper is called a "candy." A shipment is counted by candies.

In recent years, because World War II destroyed the pepper estates of Indonesia, India has enjoyed a world monopoly of that spice. The United States alone consumes around forty million pounds of pepper in a year. There is a good profit in pepper commerce for Indian estate owners, though there is some risk, too, because the vines are delicate. It will require several years for the East Indies to restore their bearing vines and India has an opportunity now to build up some economic strength in this way. Capital is needed in the new republic for many expanding kinds of business and if pepper money continues to be available, the outlook is good.

India has also given the world the combinations of spices known as curries. We are slowly developing in America a taste for such seasonings. In India there is a different combination of the required spices for each kind of food, one for fish, another for chicken, and another for lamb, to name a few. They use coriander seed which some American mothers put in apple pie; turmeric, the yellow root which we use in making pickles; the anise and cummin known in Bible times. Ginger, cinnamon, cocoanut, hot red peppers and cardamom are all on the list.

Whatever the day or the season, the Indian landscape, the Indian food bazaar, the Indian weather, the Indian road offer pleasure to the eye and the tongue of any traveler.

II. HISTORY

THE history of India, which covers so many hundreds of years, can be described in a few sentences. Invaders from many lands came at different times through the centuries. They conquered the people they found, they ruled for a while, brought their religious faiths and their skills as a contribution or a rivalry to those already existing, and were in their turn conquered by successors.

India is a very old land which has now, in a way, become young again, because it is the home of two of the newest nations recognized by international politics, the Union of India which is the Hindu state, and Pakistan, the Muslim one.

One must look back to the beginning, to prehistoric times even, and trace the story to the present to be able to understand why it is true that though India is such an ancient land, it can still also be one of the newest nations. India, the land, and India, a nation, are a part of each other, inseparable.

The history of India, up to 1947 when independence came, falls easily into four periods.

The first was the time of Aryan invasion and settlement, the early years. The written record, for North India at least, began about 600 B.C. During this time Hinduism as a religion reached a high development, fell away when Buddhism became popular, and was restored again. This period lasted to 700 A.D., or about thirteen hundred years. Then the first Muslims appeared in 712 A.D. from Arabia and conquered a Hindu king.

That was the beginning of the second historical period. The Moghuls were the most famous of all the Muslim rulers in India. Their chief opponents were the Rajputs, the warrior clans of the Hindus. The pattern of rivalry between Muslim and Hindu, which continued over twelve hundred years, was established in this period. That rivalry culminated in August, 1947, when the Hindu state, the Union of India, and the Muslim state, Pakistan, were formed.

The Moghuls were the last of the Muslims to make any significant contribution to the progress of India. When they began to decline in the early 1700s, the British East India Company, chartered by Queen Elizabeth I in 1600, was already established at several strategic points in both North and South India. They were then the only unifying force which could cope with the lawlessness and confusion that marked the decline of Moghul power.

The gradual development of the administration of India's affairs by the British East India Company, which lasted about one hundred and fifty years, was the beginning of the third historical period.

Although the men in the Company were in business and had come to India only for trade, they were experienced organizers. They knew how to manage local trouble when rulers died without leaving heirs to their thrones. The Company had a well-trained army to protect their trade. In time the army was used to protect civil administration as well.

The transfer of the control of India by this great trading Company to the government of Great Britain in 1858 began the Empire period which ended on August 15, 1947, which is India's Independence Day.

Reference in this book to "India" after 1947 is to the Hindu state, the Union of India, though there are still Muslims as well as Hindus in the civil population. Many Muslims chose to remain in India when the two new states were formed rather than to move to Pakistan.

Earlier happenings made modern India what it is. The prophet Ecclesiastes, writing in Old Testament times, said there is nothing new under the sun. Yet while the old abides, something emerges in each age for youth to consider in a new way. Here and there the names of a few men and women stand out from the multitude, because they represent some new idea or force in science, religion, or education. But even they are a product of the old on which they have built.

Such a one was Mahatma Gandhi, whose life has been excellently written by several biographers. Such a one is Pandit Jawaharlal Nehru, now India's Prime Minister. Such a one was Madame Sarojini Naidu, one of India's best-loved poets and first woman governor of a province in the new Republic.

There have been many others, both men and women. But India's story is not that of one person or a few. It is the life of all her people, her priests and princes, the warriors, the merchants, proud Brahmans and humble outcastes. It is the tale of their successes and failures, their beliefs, their good times, and the story of their children along the road of history.

4

THE EARLY YEARS, 600 B.C. – 700 A.D.

LONG AGO, before there was written history, nomadic tribes from Central Asia found the passes through the Himalaya mountains and came into India from the northwest. They were hunting new pastures for their herds and perhaps a better way of life for themselves. They had the same hopes and urges that people have nowadays to make their lives happier and more comfortable.

We have no record of how many times they tried to go through the mountain barrier, nor of how many times they failed. Himalaya means "the place of snow". The mountains are so high that some of them have always been covered with snow, and glaciers fill some of the valleys between. So those early adventurers must have tried many times before they found the way.

We know from the experiences of modern travelers that the ways between Asia and India are comparatively safe during only a few short weeks in the year. The rest of the time the passes are filled with snow, and storms higher in the mountains send great avalanches crashing down to block the road and endanger life. In the spring some of the choked snow melts away, but June is the ideal month, before the ice bridges break, to make the trip safely.

The Zogi-La Pass which leads through from Leh, the capital of Ladakh or Little Tibet, down into the valley of the Sind River in the northwestern part of India, is about 12,000 feet elevation, in a range of mountains that reach the height of Nanga Parbat, a famous peak which is 26,000 feet. Even at 12,000 feet it is difficult to breathe and Westerners particularly suffer from the thin air at that altitude.

There is no ancient record of that first successful trip to India. We do not know how difficult the journey was when the Aryan invaders first led their people down, perhaps through the Zogi-La or the now more famous Khyber Pass, beyond the snowline to the hot, rock-strewn defiles and out onto the broad grasslands which they had come seeking. We have no way of knowing how the animals felt, and whether or not their owners knew that horses would die unless their noses bled at the top of the Pass, to relieve the pressure of the height. We know only that enough people and animals survived that rugged experience to change the course of Indian history.

How surprised those early travelers would have been if they might have looked into the future! They would have learned then that the land into which they came would be called India after many hundreds of years, and that as a nation it would have in time a Zogi-La Day. The first national observance of this day took place December 7, 1948, in honor of the achievement of a crack Indian Army Regiment, the Seventh Light Cavalry, which successfully took heavy tanks over the Pass in the month of November. This, too, under fire from the enemy because it was an incident of the recent fighting in Kashmir over the question whether that former Princely State should belong to India or Pakistan.

At the celebration there was lunch for the troops. There was a program of sports, including pony races, and at the end a presentation of handsome silver cups to winners of each event. That celebration gave much pleasure to the participants and to the hundreds of people who came to watch. But it had also a sharp significance. Man had conquered another force of Nature. Man, with a machine he had thought of and built, had battled with wind and snow and had broken down another barrier separating peoples. The enormous wheels of each tank battered at the drifted snow and the rocks in the Pass. The drivers, warm and snug inside and with plenty of oxygen to breathe, were almost a part of their machines. They crossed the Pass safely. They had made a way through in winter. What they did can be done again, when needed.

Probably the only program on that far-off earlier day of the first Pass break-through was one to which the tribes were already accustomed. First they must have made camp. Then they cooked some food, and before they slept their first night in the new land they performed their simple religious ritual in worship of the only deity they knew, Brahma, Spirit, represented to them in Water and Fire and Earth and Air.

The newcomers were pleased with the country they had found beyond the mountains. Here was forest for shade, and good soil where they could grow food, much better soil than that of the dry region they had left. Here was a river, the Sind, in the valley they had followed out of the mountains, where they could get water for crops. It was a good land. They decided to wander no more.

We have learned a great deal about those early Aryans, their skills, the kind of food they liked, their wars, their religion and their customs, from their sacred books which were written from memory and word-of-mouth accounts many, many years later. These nomads were part of a greater migration out of Central Asia, which took place at that time. Some of the wanderers went west into Europe. Others went to Persia. And the third body, the restless herdsmen, gathered up their families and their animals and their priests and set out, not knowing what might be ahead. They found India, a pleasant land, waiting.

They brought a different way of life to the primitive people they found in the country. These were the aborigines, the Dravidians, a people whose past is even more obscure than that of the earliest Aryans. Scholars can tell a great deal about ancient times by reading inscriptions crudely cut on stones, by the kinds of implements a people used and by the sort of buildings they lived in. But even the scholars have little to say about the prehistoric life of the Dravidians, particularly in South India.

The early years of South Indian history are not as easily traceable as those of the North. A civilization was there, we know. Legends of cities persist and archeologists have found evidence here and there which proves an early knowledge and intelligent use of iron. Also, there are references in old writings of the North to their own invasions made in the South, beyond the central dividing line of the Vindhya hills. Other than these meagre facts the definite history of what happened in South India is not known for the years between 600 B.C. and 600 A.D.

If people who are living now could look at the history of India as if it were a wonderful play on a great stage, it would be a very fine thing indeed. What would they see?

People, first. Onto the stage from the wings would come a great procession of men and women and boys and girls, leading their animals and carrying the things they worked with, or liked best, an endless line, because India is such an old land and can count its history by centuries.

They would see kings in the procession and humble people, men who worked in the soil and men who rode proudly on horses, and merchants with their account books. They would see priests carrying altar bells, and poets with their writing materials, already beginning to set down the famous poetry and religious hymns of India.

In the course of the procession they would see the type of people gradually changing. The Hindu conquerors, the tall, fair Aryans, forced acceptance of their customs and religion on the darker-skinned aborigines called Dravidians. But they also married some of them and found themselves accepting in turn the ways of the conquered people. That was bound to be, and in time the descendants of that fusion of blood and acceptance of each other's gods and ways of living became the ancestors of the modern Hindu race. This did not come about all at once. It took centuries of time, going by quietly or stormily when there were battles.

It was during this time of beginnings that the caste system, peculiar to India, developed. The idea originated with the Hindu priests, who, historians think, had become alarmed about the races intermingling. They thought that by dividing the people into classes and making laws to prevent marriage between them, it would keep the races apart. There were only four castes in the beginning.

The highest caste was that of the priests themselves, the *Brahmans*, the representatives of Brahma, the All-Wise, All-Knowing, or God. Nowadays not all Brahmans are priests, but they keep their status as the highest caste, unless, of course, they have become Christian. Many of them have. In America the word Brahman has come to mean those people who are very brilliant and wise and somewhat exclusive in their learning.

Because the priests assumed for themselves the right to make laws, kings were classed with soldiers, and they formed together the next caste, known as *Kshatriyas*. Much later all the Rajput clans claimed membership in this second caste.

Merchants and farmers, the *Vaisyas*, were the third order, and below them were the *Sudras*, the slaves and servants of all, the conquered people.

Hindus believe that the priestly class sprang from the head of Brahma, the warriors from his hands, the farmers and merchants from his waist and the lower classes from his feet.

If the only purpose of the caste system was to prevent intermarriage of the newcomers with the Dravidians, it did not succeed. But the introduction of the caste system was certainly an attempt to make the Dravidians feel the power of their conquerors.

It was inevitable, as time went on, that the first invaders should themselves be invaded. More Aryans found their way through the mountain passes and a special class of warriors began to develop because the people had to fight for their rights to lands which they had begun to call home. The population grew and spread and small communities became larger ones and each warrior leader had his own following of loyal people.

Gradually, as each of these men developed larger armies and more power, small independent kingdoms grew up. All worshipped in about the same way and the kingdoms were all formed by people of the same blood.

There were sixteen such small independent states in North India, between the Himalayas and the Vindhya hills, at the time history first began to be written down, about 600 B.C. These, taken together, were the nucleus of the First Empire of which King Asoka, a Maurya Prince, was the best known and longest remembered ruler. The names of other Maurya kings, the lands they won and lost, and their great deeds, with those of Asoka, are to be found in old religious writings of the Buddhists.

Buddhism was a separate, new religion, which developed about the time that history first began to be written. Its founder, a young prince who lived in the years

567 to 487 B.C., left his father's court and began to teach a small group of friends his idea of the best way to live. He later became known as Gautama Buddha, the second name meaning Wise One. He taught that a man ruled his own destiny by the way he lived and not by following a ritual prescribed by a priest. Self-control, kindness to all men, and reverence for life in every creature were his three chief principles of conduct. It was a simple faith and the people were ready for something new. Hinduism had become, by that time, a religion for the priests and the higher castes, the number of which had increased from the original four.

A great deal later, in the eleventh century A.D., Hinduism experienced a great revival and Buddhism died away. But many Buddhistic principles were incorporated into the Hindu teachings and are traceable there to this day.

There were other records besides those of the Buddhists. We know about some of those early happenings because Greek historians also collected the details in their writings about the visit of Alexander, their great king, to India in 327 B.C. It was more than a visit. He, too, changed the course of Indian history. The Greek influence can still be traced in Indian art and architecture in the northwest.

Alexander spent three years in India, fighting the sixteen Indian kings. When he returned to Greece he left garrisons of his soldiers in the captured cities of what is now known as the Punjab, the Land of the Five Rivers. He meant to return and make those cities into a colony of the empire he was building. But he died of malaria in 323 B.C., a young general of thirty-three who wept because there were no more worlds to conquer.

The First Empire

When the news of Alexander's death reached India one of the stronger kings of the sixteen, Chandra Gupta, led the rest in a revolt against the Greek garrisons and drove them out. Then he united all of North India under one rule, his own, and that was the beginning of the First Indian Empire.

The Greek writers' accounts give many details about life during the First Empire. By that time the people had found precious metals and jewels and had learned how to make useful and ornamental things from them. They had beautiful bowls of gold and of burnished copper set with shining stones. They lived in wooden houses, some of them two stories in height. They rode richly decorated elephants to battle. The soldiers fought with spears and bows and arrows. They had developed a good system of government by which to maintain law and order over a large stretch of country. They were religious—Buddhists now for the most part.

Asoka, who reigned from 272 B.C. to his death in 231 B.C., is the most famous ruler of the First Empire. He was the third of his family in the dynasty and under him was united the largest part of India ever to come under one government until August, 1947. Even British India under the Viceroys was never as large in extent of territory. The Mauryas held all of North India and the country south of the Vindhya hills as far as the modern city of Madras. This in itself would be something to remember about the third century, B.C., but the most wonderful thing about King Asoka's reign was the man himself.

In the beginning he ruled much as other kings before him had done, and he went to war as they did to increase his lands. Buddhism was then the most popular religious faith in India but Asoka did not become active in it until, in the sixteenth year of his reign, he led his armies into battle for still another conquest. He was fighting in the kingdom which is now the province of Orissa, immediately south of Bengal, on the east coast of India. The people there were brave and fought well, but many were taken captive or killed. When the king saw the destruction he had caused, the famine and disease which always follow fighting, he realized for the first time that all wars make unnecessary suffering.

As a result he became a deeply religious man. He not only followed the Buddhist faith himself but did everything he could to spread its teachings. He believed in peaceful relations with all men and in religious tolerance; no taking of life even for food; renunciation of wealth; the exercise of patience and wisdom and generosity.

That all his subjects might know of his change of heart and that they might follow his example, King Asoka drew up a series of royal edicts in which he outlined his own ideas for obeying the teachings of Buddha. There were no newspapers in those days, none of the means of communication which we now have. But there were skilled artisans who could carve words on stone. So the king appointed official letter cutters to do the work.

Twenty or more of King Asoka's stone inscriptions have been found and translated by modern scholars. Some of the teachings are good for adults and children alike, even to this day. It should not be too hard for any age to be kind to animals, to show respect to parents, teachers and elders, and to speak the truth. Some of the stones have been found in walls of buildings. Others were set on their own special foundations. One such inscription near the scene of the Orissa battles is done in three columns and above it is an elephant which archeologists believe is one of the earliest known examples of this kind of sculpture. Sometimes the smoothed surface of a wayside rock was used for lettering the edicts.

The pillars erected in various parts of Asoka's empire had another significance, for, in addition to the edicts they bore, some of them were made of iron, proving the ancient knowledge in India of the use of that metal.

All of the edicts were done in Prakit, which was then

the language of the people, as opposed to Sanskrit which was the language of scholars.

Some of the proposed reforms were startling. Nobody before had cared about looking after the aged. Nobody before had worried about bad relationships between servants and their masters, or between people of different castes. No other king had created a special office among his ministers to see that these new ideas of social welfare for the whole country were carried out.

There was still another forceful new thought in Asoka's words. For the first time a king was saying that the power of a state should be used to make life better for its people, rather than to get more power for itself. It was an idea which was to be remembered and honored two thousand years later when India became a modern nation.

After the death of King Asoka in 231 B.C., the empire he had built up was never again as large in territory nor was it as powerful. His last descendant was killed in 184 B.C. by an army chieftain who set up a dynasty of his own.

From that time until the rise of the Rajputs between 650 A.D. and 700, the history of Aryan advance in India is one of battles back and forth across the map of India. Princes whose names are forgotten headed small empires which lasted for only a few generations. Then their lands were absorbed by another state of larger dimensions.

Some of these men were Buddhists. Some who had

been Buddhists at first reverted to the ancient Hindu faith. This happened because there was a religious struggle at the time, led by the Hindu priests, against the increasing popularity of Buddhism. They tried, by absorbing some of the Buddhist teachings, by creating new gods of their own and by increasing the number of castes, to make the old religion more attractive.

5

THE RAJPUTS AND THE MOGHULS, 700–1700 A.D.

IF ONE WISHED to describe this period of Indian history in a few words, one would be *grandeur*. Another would be *cruelty*. A third would be *progress*. These apply alike to the lives and the acts of Rajput and Moghul.

The true origin of the Rajputs is in doubt. Historians agree that they belonged originally to several different races. According to tradition and legend the ancestry of some of the Rajput clans dates back to early Aryan chieftains. Others had their beginning among the wild tribes of Central Asia who successively invaded India in the early centuries after the birth of Christ. There are even some of almost wholly Dravidian ancestry.

All Rajputs seem to have had one thing in common, their spirit of adventure and zeal in battle. When castes were begun, they all, regardless of racial origin, claimed the status of warriors. Each soldier was required to keep a horse on which he rode to battle. A Rajput would never fight on foot.

The Rajputs have never followed any other religion but Hinduism.

The most famous of these clans lived in the dry, sandy country of western India, along the coast and extending north into the Sind desert, called Rajputana nowadays, and in Central India. They first claimed historical attention in the middle of the seventh century after Christ.

After the death of King Harsha in 660 A.D.—he was one of Asoka's most illustrious successors—the lands he had held under one rule, Buddhist in character, again became independent. But not for long. By fighting and conquering these small states, the Rajputs became masters of Northern India and held it until the coming of the Muslims.

One or another of these warring Rajput families had extended their power south into the plateau country of the Deccan, and for a second time most of India, but not all, was brought under one government.

The story of South India between the seventh and eleventh centuries A.D. is partly parallel with the activities of the Rajputs there. In 620 A.D. a powerful Prince of the clan known as the Chalukyas ruled the whole of the peninsula south of the Narbada River, which with the Vindhya hills, divides India into North and South. During this period the Ellora temple was carved out of solid rock in a cave. It remains one of the finest examples of Hindu architecture and testifies to their knowledge of the science of physics.

For the first time stone was used in making temples and palaces instead of bricks.

It was a period of advancement and prosperity and an important one in Indian history because of the further development of trade with other countries. It is recorded in the works of Greek and Roman historians as well as in Indian writings that trade flourished between India and Egypt and India and Rome many years before the time of Christ and on into the first century, though much of it was by land routes. Coins of the Emperor Nero's time have been found in excavating old cities in South India. How could this money have got there unless it had been used in payment for goods purchased?

During the period of the Rajputs' greatest power, between 650 and 1100 A.D., Hinduism completely replaced Buddhism which gradually died out in India, though it was spread in China and Japan by loyal monks. These were the years of the Rajputs' greatest glory, too, when deeds of chivalry and romance created their modern pride of race. But the bitter rivalries and jealousies of individual princes made union under one Rajput government impossible. They were not able to act together on anything. That was the principal reason why, when the Muslims came, their conquest was so apparently easy. They had to fight only small forces, one at a time, thus saving their own reserves.

If the individual Rajput states had united, they would have been stronger in their defense and thus again the history of India might have been changed.

The word Moghul has come to mean, in our vivid American speech, something large or elegant or forceful of its kind. An American railroad named one of its great engines *The Moghul*. Businessmen, in speaking of another who has been successful in a spectacular way, who has piled up a great fortune, or is at the head of a large enterprise, call him a Moghul. The word originally was only the Arabic spelling of a racial name, Mongol.

The Moghul rulers of India, who began with Prince Babar in 1525 A.D. and ended with Aurungzeb in 1707, had Mongol blood in their ancestry and they were followers of Islam, which means literally "submission to the will of God." Those who live by its teachings are called Muslims.

This religion, begun by a man called Mohammed in Arabia in about the year 630 A.D., is a fighting one. The early Muslims believed in making converts by first conquering a people in battle and then forcing them to accept their religion. A Muslim believes that if he should die in battle he will be rewarded by being taken into Heaven to enjoy a blissful state of existence, with no wars in it, forevermore.

The teachings of Mohammed are contained in the Koran, the sacred book of Islam. The Muslims worship one Supreme God and revere Mohammed as His Prophet. Their priestly offices do not correspond to those of the Hindus. Their preachers and teachers are called *maulvi* and the official who gives the call to prayer daily from a mosque tower is called the *muezzin*. There is no caste division in this religion.

Mecca, in Arabia, is the sacred city of the whole world of Islam. At prayers the kneeling worshipper faces in its direction, wherever he is.

The first Muslims to force a way into India through the Himalayan passes were Arabs who, in 712 A.D., pillaged and burned as they came and conquered the district of Sind, the Rajputs' home country. The shrines of the Hindus angered them, as an offense to God. The young Muslim leader fell into disfavor in Arabia when he went back and never returned to India. The people of Sind resumed their Rajput-Hindu ways, absorbing the few Arabs still remaining, and thus added the blood of still another race to their own mixed ancestry.

Mohammed's teachings had meantime spread to Turkey and it was during the conquest of Sind that the Turkish believers of the sect seized authority throughout the Muslim world. In the beginning of the thirteenth century (1206) they took Delhi in India for their capital and five dynasties reigned there until the coming of Babar, the first of the Moghuls.

Through his mother Babar was a descendant of Timur, the cruel Asiatic conqueror called "The Scourge of God". Through his father, who was a Prince of Ferghana, now a part of the Soviet Union, Babar was a Turk. All of his life he had been a soldier of fortune, a man schooled in war and political strategy. By 1525 he had become ruler of Afghanistan, a kingdom in the hills on the northwest border of India.

The lands of the five Turkish dynasties, ruled from their capital at Delhi, had gradually dwindled. The great kingdom which had once extended as far south as the Deccan was lost. Princes of other small, nearby kingdoms had re-won their independence. The last king of the fifth dynasty was scarcely crowned before the Rajput princes revolted in one more effort to restore the government of all North India to the Hindus. A messenger from Delhi rode swiftly to Kabul, Babar's capital, with the news. It was a moment Babar had anxiously anticipated. He was ready.

He brought his bowmen, his foot soldiers, his strong, hill-trained troops, down through the river valleys and the plains of India and fought victoriously at Panipat, a place about fifty miles north of modern Delhi. A peaceful, co-operative village scheme is going on there now, where one of the decisive battles of the world once scorched the earth. It was decisive in that it was the last stand of the Hindus, led by the Rajputs, to regain their old power. It was the beginning of Moghul rule in India.

It was also the beginning of the long feud between the Hindus and the Muslims which was to end, in 1947, in the division of political government into two sovereign states. Now there is Pakistan, the Muslim state, and the Union of India, the Hindu state. Most of the Muslims now living in India or in Pakistan are descendants of the Moghuls who conquered at Panipat. A few are descendants of Hindus who allowed themselves to be converted to the Muslim faith at the time of the Moghul supremacy. In other words, they have become meat-eaters, and in Hindu eyes worthy of contempt. All orthodox Hindus are vegetarians. Only those of the lowest castes, or those who are called untouchable because they are considered beneath all caste level, are meat-eaters.

Babar was forty-four years old in that year of victory, 1526, and he was to live in the Indian plain for four more years. He founded the city of Agra as his new capital and he was the grandfather of Akbar.

As King Asoka stands out in his age, the Emperor Akbar, reigning in India at the time Queen Elizabeth I ruled in England, is the central figure of this Moghul period which ushered in a change in the whole political history of India.

Through his grandfather Akbar received a mixture of gifts, in both mind and body. He was energetic. He loved justice. He levied fair taxes and these were subject to readjustment from time to time.

Akbar began a new system of official appointments. There was no religious preferment in assigning men to different offices. He gave positions to any who were qualified to do the particular work that was needed, even though the man might be a Hindu. During his entire reign the conquered people were not oppressed as they had been during the period when the five Turkish dynasties were in power.

The tolerance of Akbar in choice of officials led to the creation of a new language. It was a combination of the official speech of the Moghul court–Persian–and the speech of the bazaar–Hindi. The latter was the Sanskrit which had changed with usage to include many provincial words. The new language, which developed because some of Akbar's officers were of the court and some were of the people, was called Urdu or Hindustani. That is why the spoken language of North India before independence was one with words of different racial origins. Nowadays Hindi–of one root, Sanskrit–is the official language of all India.

Under Akbar India enjoyed religious tolerance for the first time. Muslims are allowed four wives so he had a Christian wife, Miriam, whose tomb is not far from his in Agra; two were Rajput princesses, Hindus, one of them the sister of the ruler of Jaipur State; a fourth was his Turkish wife about whom very little is known. This was his royal way of teaching the Indian people to live peaceably with each other, even though their religious beliefs were so different. He even tried, in his later life, to form a new religion, a combination of the best in Hinduism and Islam, but he found that that was impossible.

Wherever the Moghuls went they were great gardeners and truly made roses bloom in the desert. Babar had introduced the Persian water wheel, known in his old home in Kabul, as a means of making gardens in dry places. In Kashmir, in Lahore, in Delhi and in Agra this line of famous kings planted gardens filled with sparkling rivulets of water, many trees and their beloved roses. These gardens have now become public parks where all the people may go to enjoy their beauty and to rest in the shade.

The whole period of Moghul rule was marked by rich material possessions. Their clothing, the furniture of their palaces, the paintings, the palace buildings themselves were rich in color and artistry. Precious stones, which have since been removed purposely or looted, were a part of the inlaid decoration of marble palace walls. The renowned Koh-i-noor diamond was one of the treasures handed down in this family of princes. It eventually became one of the crown jewels of Queen Victoria in England. There were many stories about the origin of this beautiful stone. Its name means "mountain of light". Some say it was a gift from a Rajput queen to the Emperor Babar when he had spared her family in battle. Others claim it was given to Shah Jahan, grandson of Akbar, by the vizier of Golconda, where the South India diamond mines are still being worked.

It was Shah Jahan, reigning in the years 1627 to 1658, who built the Taj Mahal, which all the world knows as the tomb of Mumtaz Mahal, his wife. The story of this building sounds like a fairy tale. India and the whole world were searched for materials for its adornment. Italians came from Europe to draw the design. Mosaic workers came from Persia. Marble was brought from the quarries in Jaipur State and jade from China. It took twenty-two years to complete the tomb, and twenty thousand men worked at one time or another on its construction. It is one of the most beautiful buildings in the world.

There is a pierced marble screen around the tomb which is as thin and fine as if it were a lacy fabric. The marble walls have been worn to velvet smoothness inside by the many hands of reverent visitors in years gone by. Green lawns spread on either side of a pool of water to great gates and there is a red sandstone mosque on right and left of the tomb. A black marble mate to the Taj was begun just opposite it, across the Jumna River, but before it could be completed, the Emperor died and was buried beside his wife in the white tomb.

Though Mumtaz Mahal has been dead for more than three hundred years, one speaks softly in the place. It has a different look at different times of the day, at sunrise, noon, sunset or under the clear Indian moonlight, but the effect of its beauty is the same. Lotuses grow in the pool, and there are tall evergreens planted beside it. When the shadows fall in late afternoon there are two tombs, one of them a reflection in the still water.

Shah Jahan was called "The Magnificent". He was the most popular of the Moghul rulers and even more tolerant toward all religions than Akbar had been.

The reign of Shah Jahan was also more notable than the others' for its luxury and splendor. He might have been given the title of "The Builder" as well, for, in addition to commissioning the erection of the great tomb, he moved his capital back to Delhi and built there the fort and the mosque, the Jama Masjid. Times were prosperous and most of the fighting for territory went on in the plateau country of the South, called the Deccan, where his son Aurangzeb was the governor.

Babar's reasons for moving the capital to Agra, when he became the first Moghul ruler, seem obscure. Delhi was worn and shabby after so many years of fighting and perhaps he had a desire to enjoy a place which he himself had planned. In returning to Delhi, it was natural that Shah Jahan should follow the general pattern of the buildings which he had known all his life in Agra.

The fort which he built at Delhi is very similar to the one at Agra. They are built of red sandstone, aged now to a lovely rose-pink. The Delhi fort is known as the Parana Qila, meaning "old fort". Inside its garrisoned walls was a small city, with a palace, an armory, housing for a large staff, and stables for the royal elephants.

There was a system of fountains and baths in the palace which were filled with perfumed water. The decoration of the great Hall of Audience was done in gold leaf on enormous creamy marble pillars. This cloistered place opened onto a large court planted with lawn and gardens.

In Shah Jahan's last years his four sons began quarreling as to the succession. It was Aurangzeb who made his father a prisoner in the Jasmine Tower at Agra Fort for seven years. He then became the last of the Moghul emperors upon Shah Jahan's death in 1658.

Aurangzeb lived in the traditional splendor of the Moghuls, but he was a religious fanatic and he wrecked completely all that his family had accomplished through religious forbearance. He destroyed the Hindu temple of Vishnu at Benares. At Madura, in South India, he built a mosque above the ruins of another temple and buried the images of the gods beneath its pavement so that they would be constantly trampled upon by the feet of Muslims coming in to pray. He fell out with the Rajput subjects again, and another angry sect of Hindus, the Mahrattas, revolted.

In spite of all these things the Moghul Empire was greatest in territory under the rule of this strange prince, who had roamed the country in his younger days disguised as a religious devotee.

After the death of Aurangzeb in 1707, there was no one strong enough to keep the restless clans united. The kingdom founded by Babar, which had flourished so gloriously in the time of Akbar and Shah Jahan, began to break apart. Many provincial governors set up their own small separate states in Bengal, in the Deccan and in Oudh.

This was the time, in 1739, when the famous Peacock Throne was taken from the fort in Delhi to Persia by a sacking army under Nadir, the Shah. Guides now point out only the place where it used to stand in the Hall of Audience. It was an enormous golden chair, measuring six feet by four and having six legs. Two peacocks with tails expanded formed the back. The canopy above, set with diamonds and emeralds and rubies, had a fringe of pearls. The peacocks' feathers were inlaid with precious stones so as to appear in natural peacock colors.

It was a fabulous throne, out of a fabulous era in Indian history, truly a time of grandeur and cruelty and progress.

6

THE ENGLISH EAST INDIA COMPANY, 1611–1858

TWO THINGS were significant at the beginning of this part of Indian history. One was trade, developing very fast between India and the rest of the world. The other was the unsettled condition of the country due to the decline of the Moghuls.

Two things were significant at the close of this period. One was trade, developing even faster and much better organized. The other was the appearance of a new government, coming peacefully, but making India a part of a foreign state.

The development of trade between different parts of India and the outside world had been gradually growing over a long period of time. In the fifth century after Christ a Chinese historian, Fa Hien, recorded an ocean journey in an Indian ship which he made from a port in Orissa, Asoka's ancient land on the east coast of India, to the island of Ceylon and on to China through the Malacca Straits. The line of kings to which Asoka belonged, the Mauryas, included "the Eastern Seas" as part of their domain.

Indian sailors had early learned navigation. They were boldly voyaging out into the Arabian Sea and the Indian Ocean long before Europeans did anything but hug the coastline, because of fear of pirates. Throughout the changing fortunes of Hindu power in South India the ocean trade routes were steadily maintained. It was not until the Portuguese came at the end of the fifteenth century that there was any dispute of right to these routes, or talk of monopoly.

The Zamorin, ruler of Calicut, a port on the west coast of India and center of the cotton industry, opposed the Portuguese claim and two battles were fought over it, in 1503 and 1509, which the Indians lost. Naval historians feel that these battles should be included in tracing the course of India's subsequent history. How different, they ask, would India's progress have been if she had had no hindrance in developing her sea power? It is one of those big "ifs" which we meet in the history of any country.

India was the first land to grow and use cotton. When the ocean routes were first cautiously explored between India and Egypt and Rome, cotton cloth was one of the articles of trade. Fine cotton material was much prized for garments by princesses in the courts of the Moghuls. Muslins from Dacca in Bengal were part of the cargoes of sailing ships in the early days of English foreign trade and later of American commerce in the early nineteenth century. Calico, the fine-sprigged cotton of which dresses were made in our Civil War period, received its name from the town of Calicut.

But it was spices, then grown abundantly in India, which had a more important effect on the history of the whole world, and we are still seeing the industry unfold in the East Indies. Spices as a world commodity had a particular influence on Indian and American history. Their value caused the early explorers to go avoyaging on a search for a shorter route to India and so, in 1492, Columbus sailed and found America. Vasco da Gama, the Portuguese, went the other way, round the Cape of Good Hope, and came to the pepper country on the Malabar Coast of India on May 20, 1498. He had been sailing almost a year. This is an important date to remember for it brought India and Europe together by sea.

There was more than wealth in the spice business in those early days. There was comfort and pleasure for the purchasers. Before the use of ice, spices helped to preserve meats. They were used in the making of perfumes and for scenting the breath. Cardamom seed is offered to casual callers in India quite as often as *pan.*

India had cinnamon, too, in the time when trade was developing though nowadays the Island of Ceylon produces more of it.

The Dutch followed the Portuguese round Africa to the East and eventually became masters of the East Indies.

It was because of the soaring price of pepper, which had become a Dutch monopoly, that the British East India Company was formed in London by some far-seeing businessmen for the purpose of direct trade with India. Queen Elizabeth I granted them a charter in 1600. In the following two hundred years the Company established itself successfully in several different strategic points in India while the power of the Moghuls rose and fell. That is why 1611, when the first trading post was actually established, is given as a date for the beginning of this period of history, even though it was another hundred years before the death of Aurangzeb, last of the Moghul dynasty.

Each settlement of the East India Company was called a factory, from the word "factor", meaning an agent. It was their policy in the beginning to stay as close as possible to the sea, to lessen expense of transfer of goods and for the protection afforded them by the nearness of their ships.

The city of Madras grew up around the first factory settled in India after Queen Elizabeth's charter was granted.

Calcutta, on the Hooghly River in Bengal, was settled because one of the Company factors, Job Charnock, liked the locality. The land was a grant to him by the Emperor Aurangzeb. But it was not a happy choice because of the unhealthy, steamy climate and poor Job has been roundly condemned these three hundred years.

A French East India Company was also organized and made its headquarters at Pondicherry on the east coast, which is still a tiny French possession in these modern times. Its early governors had an idea that conquest would give them all of South India. They were disappointed.

In order to protect their factories and maintain their trade rights against French, Dutch and Portuguese competition, it was necessary for the British East India Company to raise and keep an army of Indian troops with British officers. Later they were obliged to use that army to defend their very right to stay in India. In the South the French hoped, by making terms with the Indian rulers of small states, to drive out the English. In Bengal the local princes were annoyed because the Company was interfering in some of their mistreatment of the people. The Englishmen demanded fair dealing for everyone.

By 1773 the country was in complete confusion, following the loss of a central government with the decline of the Moghuls. In a few small Princely States where the rulers had shown themselves too weak to govern or where there was no heir, regents had been placed and British Residents appointed by the Company to keep law and order so that business might proceed. Thus the Company found itself with a new duty, that of administration. It was a gradual development, coming in a way that no one had planned or foreseen.

Inasmuch as the Company was rapidly developing into an administrative body in India, the Parliament of England decided that it would be better to have India officially governed. In that year, 1773, the Regulating Act was passed, which provided that henceforth the British Government would appoint governors-general for India and that the British East India Company should receive a grant of money, ostensibly to reimburse it for expense incurred in protecting its business treaties.

It should be noted, for the sake of further understanding the modern political structure in India, that at the time this Act was passed, there was no possible way for the Indian people to express their wishes in the matter. They were not consulted. What was done was thought to be for the best interests of all—to keep order in the country and thus to protect life and property.

A succession of governors came out from England, each serving a few years. Lord Cornwallis, who had fought for his government in the American Revolution, was one of them. Each tried to reform existing systems to improve conditions. Some were good, some were weak, some were exceptionally brilliant administrators. The names of many streets and institutions in modern Calcutta, which became the seat of government, are a tribute to their service in office. Together, they welded India into a group of well-managed provinces. The Department of Public Works, the telegraph system, the postal system, irrigation by canals, railways and schools were started.

Side by side with the organization of provincial governments, some of the powerful Princely States, great Rajput Houses, and others were growing in wealth and power. They exist today, though with somewhat curtailed independence, because they have come into the Union of India.

Then, when it began to appear that trade and business might go along unhindered, the Indian soldiers of the Company's army rebelled. There were many reasons. The Hindu priests, who were afraid of the effect of the new telegraph system, the post office and educational institutions on old religious customs, were glad to plot with disgruntled people wherever they found them. They also traded on the superstitions of the people and told exciting stories of violation of caste by the British. The railways and other improvements were not designed to help the Indians but to hurt them, they said.

The soldiers themselves had other dissatisfactions, too, about wages, and the prospect of being sent out of the country, whereby their caste might be broken. The result was an uprising against their English officers, simultaneously at Meerut and at Delhi and Lucknow and Cawnpore and in several places in Bengal and Central India. It is known in history as the great Indian Mutiny of 1857.

Out of it grew the incorporation of India into the British Empire, in November of 1858, when Queen Victoria was declared the ruler of India. For a third time a large part of India was united under one government, with the exception of the small bit owned by the French in the South, and Goa which belonged to Portugal. But it was a foreign rule, as that of the Moghuls had been, and it, too, was destined to pass away.

7

IN THE BRITISH EMPIRE, 1858–1947

A GOOD PHRASE to describe this period of Indian history would be "India under the Viceroys". *Vice* means in-place-of and *roy* comes from the French word for king. Viceroys were the men who governed India for the English Crown.

Following the Act of the British Parliament in 1858 when India was taken over formally by Great Britain, Queen Victoria issued a Proclamation. It promised two things. About religious tolerance the Queen said, "We declare it to be our royal will and pleasure that none be in any wise favoured, none molested or disquieted, by reason of their religious faith or observances; . . ." About service in government offices the Proclamation read, "And it is further our will that, so far as may be, our subjects, of whatever race or creed, be fully and impartially admitted to offices in our service, the duties of which they may be qualified by their education, ability and integrity, duly to discharge".

There were other matters in the paper but these two were most significant. The first one explains why British officials were not able to interfere when there were riots between Muslim and Hindu.

The second one explains how Indians could take over a complicated government and administer it when the time came. They had been trained for it. They had participated in it before independence.

Queen Victoria appointed Lord Canning as her first Viceroy. He made a tour about India, seeking to straighten out the confusion in many localities following the end of the Mutiny. Much credit is owed him that he was able to establish a government again.

The early years under the Viceroys were a period of development and growth in organization. Relations with border tribes were strengthened. The army was restored to usefulness and increased in size. Most of the Princely States had been loyal to Great Britain at the time of the Mutiny. Lord Canning gave them public honor with decorations and recognition of their friendship.

It was not until 1877 that Queen Victoria was made Empress of India by an Act of Parliament. A magnificent durbar was held at Delhi, and a proclamation read, acknowledging the new title.

In 1880 Lord Ripon was made Viceroy. He was first to recognize the value of interesting the Indian people in government. Accordingly, in 1882, he introduced a new system of local management under the Self-Government Act, by the creation of District and Municipal Boards. These local boards were given authority over roads, sanitation, primary education and public buildings. They were also given the right to raise money by taxes to maintain public works. There is early mention of income tax for this purpose.

Meantime missionaries of many faiths were at work in the country and it is a familiar truth that wherever they go, the people they educate become anxious to rule themselves. With knowledge, self-respect is increased.

It was not a new thing when independence was granted to India in 1947. Agitation for it had been going on for years, and slowly, government and the people came together.

This was aided by the passage of the Indian Councils Act in 1909 which provided for a Legislative Council, with the same purpose as those for Municipal and District management. By the new Act Indians could now elect their own representatives to sit in provincial legislatures. Above these was to be the Viceroy's Legislative Council, which would have the responsibility of making the laws for all of India.

But this was not enough for the political reformers

who began to clamor, a decade later, for an Indian-governed India. They thought Great Britain was too slow in deciding which was the right time to give them independence. They forgot about Japan, waiting to step into England's place. They refused to fear possible internal trouble between Hindus and Muslims if participation in the new government was not safeguarded for every community. There were other problems of financial credit and of organization to be carefully thought out.

When it became evident that the only solution was to set up two sovereign States, because the Muslims were still afraid they would be suppressed under a Hindu government, it was finally arranged.

This plan had not been accomplished easily. In the twenty-five years preceding freedom from the rule of a foreign power many Indians had practiced "non-co-operation", a form of striking against the existing government. There had been appeasement and interviews and imprisonments. There had been commissions sent from England to India. There had been delegates sent from India to round table discussions in England. There had been a succession of Viceroys.

In the end there was Lord Louis Mountbatten, the tall British sailor, cousin of King George V, a wise, kind and audacious man, who surprised everybody by bringing the long-drawn-out negotiations to a head much more quickly than anyone had thought possible. And he was the last Viceroy.

There was one unforeseen result of independence. A great exodus of people began, of Hindus out of Pakistan and of Muslims out of India, all trying to get to what they thought was safety in their new states. The movement had not been planned for and it happened almost overnight. Families loaded household goods on carts and started out, walking. Others jammed railroad stations, trying to get places on overcrowded trains.

They lost the savings of a lifetime. They lost title to the lands and houses they were leaving behind. Thousands lost their lives because the old Hindu-Muslim animosity flamed again. The confusion gave individuals an easy opportunity to work off old hates. Whole villages were massacred before the trouble died down. There was terrifying fear everywhere.

The situation caused strained relations between the two new states at a time when they most needed to be at peace. Thousands of displaced people needed food and medicine and shelter and work at a time when the organization of the two new governments required every official's attention. If quick military action had not been available a really serious civil war might have spread throughout India, but skilled strategy kept it localized in upper India. Even with that it was a time of chaos, of heartbreak and of wasteful destruction.

8

THE PEOPLE

THE HISTORY of any country is the story of the life of all the people. They make the country what it is, for good or bad, for progress or decay, whether it is a few people in the government, or many, as in a democracy or a republic. The manner of government is only the combined thought of the people in office, who have the power to make the laws and to say how the country shall develop. This has always been true though it was not accepted in ancient times when a king was believed to have all power vested in himself. But when the United States became a nation in its own right, it was immediately agreed that the powers of government came from the consent and the thought of the people.

We are now seeing this come true in India, with a few differences, one of them being the identification of a political group by its religion.

The names of many famous men, both Indian and English, are a part of the story of India. Many books have been written about them. But each man represents the kind of time he lived in, so it is not his story alone. He is the product of the way all of the people were thinking and acting and feeling at the time he lived. He is the product of his era and all the people make the era.

Who are the people who have made the story of India from the beginning until now?

They are very like Americans. They are friendly. They are artistic. They have exceptional dramatic ability. Even the little children show this. Many are good students. More are successful businessmen. They love their families. A few are becoming leaders and are developing the sort of qualities seen in the character of King Asoka. One also finds among Indians some of the same bad qualities which Americans have. In other words, they are PEOPLE, with the usual kinds of character which all human beings have.

There is no one thing which makes a people or a nation different from any other. It is a combination of things. Seasons and winds and mountains are a few, which is another way of saying that climate and geography have a great deal to do with the way people work, what they eat, how fast they learn, how they treat each other, what is their health and their general welfare.

It is because of climate that the people of India have brown skin, for they belong to the Caucasian race as do we in America. But living for generations under the hot eastern sun has darkened the skin pigment which makes complexions dark or fair. The people who live in Kashmir and Afghanistan are noticeably much fairer.

The two chief differences between people of the Eastern Hemisphere and the Western Hemisphere, or between the dwellers in India and those in the United States, are the traits influenced by climate and those affected by religion.

The climate of India is not generally invigorating, except in the mountains and the short cold weather period of three or four months on the plains of North India. For that reason the development of many economic enterprises has not been as swift as in the West.

In America we are taught to be religious but we are allowed freedom in the way we express our devotion to a loving God and His teachings. In the Hindu religious law each person's way of life is prescribed. There is a ceremonial for eating and drinking, for almost every waking act. These are found in the Code of Manu, an old religious book which dictates the rules for each caste. It was also used as a guide by the British East India Company when the time came to draw up regulations for governing the country, because it contains a great deal of public and civil law.

The many religious rules in Hindu worship seem only to increase the fear of the gods if there should be innocent disobedience. Many ceremonials of worship have become little more than offering of gifts to angry gods to appease them and ward off some kind of harm.

Racially the people of India are a mixture, as Americans are, and the association and mingling of the races in the East came about in somewhat the same way that it did in America—invasion or colonization first, in a search for new homes; then business. After that the comparison changes. Americans became united in one nation long before Indians did. One reason for our earlier achievement of the national goal is our speech. Nearly everyone spoke the same mother tongue in the early days of the American colonies. In India, North and South were settled by different people, and their languages did not spring from the same roots, so that even to this day the people from the South, speaking *Tamil* or *Kanarese*, and those who speak Urdu or Hindi, from the North, must converse in English to be understood, or through an interpreter, a man who knows both tongues. That is not a common accomplishment.

There are eighty principal tongues spoken in India and many provincial dialects stem from them, so that a common speech is very desirable to bring all the people together. The new government has chosen Hindi for the official language of the nation. No matter which one eventually becomes official it is a step in the right direction to choose one to follow, for the speech barrier has been another factor in keeping India in separate small political divisions.

There is a little tag which helps to identify the two chief races in India, the one from the other, and that is, "All Hindus are Indian, but not all Indians are Hindus." The Hindu is a descendant of the union of early invaders with the people they found in the country. The Muslim is the descendant of the one-time conquerors of Hindu India who remained in the country to become the chief rivals of Hinduism for supremacy in everything. That rivalry is another important reason why it took so long for India to become a nation. Since 1947, the Muslims have had their own state, Pakistan, though many of them, four million, elected to remain in India and live under the Hindu government. They had their good reasons. The individual Muslim and Hindu are often great friends. And there were business and property and family responsibilities which made the move unattractive.

In the North there are Sikhs and Rajputs and the Mahrattas and the Jains, all of them Hindus or of Hindu origin. The Rajputs are the descendants of the first warriors who all claimed to be *Kshatriyas* when the people were classified, though some of them are now agriculturists.

In the South the many modern dialect-speaking people, the Tamil, Telegu and Kanarese, are Hindu-Dravidian in their origin. Their own names and the names of their cities and the things they use are so different from those of the North that with only a little knowledge it is possible to tell in a story whether one is reading about the people of the North or the South, if the author has not specified. For instance, the small two-wheeled cart, the tonga, used so much in cities in the North, is known as a *bundy* in the South. The *jatka* of the South, another two-wheeler with no springs or seats—one sits on a little platform high over the wheels—is an *ekka* in the North.

Politeness and graciousness are two of the most prominent characteristics of the Indian people, no matter what caste they are, nor what their occupation is. We could afford to be like them more than we are. An Indian will never begin a conversation abruptly. He will greet you with a graceful gesture, using the word "salaam" if he is a Muslim or a Christian and "namaskar" if he is a Hindu, and ask after your health as if he meant it, and if you do not do the same he will think you very rude. There are several forms of the salaam. One may join hands and raise them to the forehead, at the same time bowing slightly. Or one may raise the right hand to the heart. In passing, one may stretch out the hand to a well-known person. Sometimes it is acceptable just to say the word "salaam" or "namaskar" as we say "hello" or "hi".

Hindus consider it a required politeness to carry

with them a small gift when they go to visit someone for the first time, particularly if that person is someone of importance. If they cannot afford anything valuable, they still take with them an offering of fruit. And likewise, when a guest comes, it is considered rude indeed, even though it is only a call and not for a meal, not to offer something to eat. For this use pan is most often presented because it is the symbol of peace and friendship. *Pan* is the chewing gum of India. Crushed arica nut mixed with shell lime is spread upon the fresh green betel leaf and rolled into a little triangle called a *bira*. The juice of the leaf itself has a puckering quality and the saliva becomes bright red in the process of chewing. It stains the mouth and in time, unless great care is taken, the teeth become black. But the Indians also have a custom of cleaning their teeth with the frayed end of a twig cut from the neem tree which has medicinal properties. Those who do this have the whitest teeth in the world.

It seems not to be generally known that India is the original home of the world's gypsies. Their own name for themselves is "romini-chal". "Romini" means "wandering man" and "chal" comes from the Hindustani word "chalna" which means "to go". The name "gypsies" is the English contraction of the word "Egyptians", although English gypsies call themselves "the Romany people" meaning those who speak the gypsy tongue. "The Romany rye" are those who like the gypsies well enough to associate with them and learn their natural speech. We have adopted the word gypsy here in the United States to mean the wandering bands of foreign-looking people who go about the country mending things and accepting farm produce for pay. The women tell fortunes and the children perch in the wagons, peering out at strangers from the hooded tops.

All gypsies reach far back to prehistoric times in India for their origin. There is definite evidence that they are descended from the tribes who would not accept Aryan dominance in those first invasions and who began then the wandering life which they have bequeathed to generation after generation since. Although they have penetrated to Persia and to Spain and England and the United States, they keep some of the same characteristics which those in India have, to this day. In India they still live by their wits, which means that they pick up a living as they wander, much the same as their brethren do in other countries. In World War II they gave a good account of themselves, fighting for India.

Gypsies are like the chameleon in their attitude toward religion. If they are in a Muslim community, then they are Muslim. If they are sojourning in a place where the Hindus are stronger, then they claim to be Hindus. Their speech is definitely of Hindustani origin, overlapped with dialects and tricks of their own, like children's "pig-Latin", inverting syllables to distract the ears of anyone who might be listening, as, for instance, calling fire *ga* instead of *ag*, which is correct.

In physique the men are muscular and wiry, never fat as many Indians become, and the women are quite beautiful. It is a strange thing that these people as a group have been able to resist all the influences which might have changed them, through so many generations.

There are Jews in South India who claim they are descendants of the tribe of Manassah carried away into captivity in Babylon. In the fourth century their leader was given a charter to occupy the land they now live on—the document has a stately language—and to make converts from the Hindus. If they ever have, it is not known.

The Parsees, followers of Zoroaster, center in and around Bombay. These people first came to India from Persia in the early thirteenth century at the time when the Middle East was being converted to Islam. They fled, just as the Pilgrims fled England, because they wanted to keep their own worship. They are called Zoroastrians from the name of one of their wise men. It is thought that Zoroaster might have been a Magus, or priest, of the same order as the Three Wise Men who came out of Persia seeking the Babe of Bethlehem on the first Christmas night long ago. The Parsees are sun worshippers and believe that the Lord of Light and Goodness carries on a ceaseless war with the Lord of Evil. They also believe that mankind was created to help the Lord of Light and that one day he will be victorious. Their sacred book is the Zend-Avesta, a collection of ritual, hymns, and an account of the creation.

Most Parsees are businessmen—merchants, bankers or heads of great industry. Their number is comparatively small in the whole of India's population, about 115,000, but they have a reputation for getting along with all the various races and religious faiths in the country and are welcome wherever they go.

Primitive tribes still live in the forests and hills of Central India as well as in the North and the South. They follow customs so purely preserved from ancient times that there can be little doubt that their origin goes back to the aborigines of India. Where they came from is still a mystery in the study of mankind. Their facial features are different from the modern Indian. They wear a different type of clothes and speak a language of their own, but their religion and worship resemble the usual forms of Hindu practice.

There is anxiety in some minds that the culture of the tribesmen will be spoiled, and the new government is taking the necessary precautions to help the tribes feel a part of the new union, yet allow them to keep their individuality as a people. Many of them gave able service in World War II, helping as scouts and in various other ways.

Another group in India, of which little has been written and more should be, is the Anglo-Indian community, the people of mixed blood. As a separate section of the Indian population, they may be about three hundred years old. They are the descendants of English, French, Portuguese and Dutch fathers and Indian mothers, a marriage custom which began at the time when traders first came to India, searching out spices and silks for Europe. English is now chiefly their mother tongue and they follow the several Christian faiths common in the country, though most belong to the Church of England.

This mixture of bloods has resulted in a class of gifted people who have created a place for themselves, economically and politically, in India. In education, in medicine and in politics they have made themselves known and in World War II provided officers in the Army, Navy and Air Force. Earlier, they gave invaluable service in a mechanical and administrative way when the railroads and telegraph lines were first being laid throughout India, as communication developed.

The captain of the first All India Olympic Hockey Team was an Anglo-Indian and seven of the players also, and the whole sports world remembers the surprise it had when India won.

The term Anglo-Indian must not be confused with the old Kipling usage which meant an Englishman serving his government in India. It was used in a colonial sense there.

Though the land of India is about one-half the size of the United States it must support five times the population that we do. Ninety percent of these 356,890,000 people—that was the figure at the census of April,

1951—live in the rural districts and eighty-five percent are not able to read, though at present there is a great interest in adult education in the villages. Parents are learning along with their children. If the mind of the people is to direct the government that mind must know what it is doing.

India is still on the long march across the world stage which began in prehistoric times.

III. INDIAN OVERTONES

A NEWCOMER to India immediately notices two things. Sound first, and then color.

India is not a quiet country. It takes a little time for a foreigner to realize that a great deal of the noise is made by human beings, in contrast to the sounds of machinery in America. There is almost unceasing speech, in the street, in shops, and even along country roads. It seems like arguing, but a great deal of it is thinking done aloud. The Indian workman is a sociable person and he talks constantly about the thing he happens to be doing at the moment.

Color in flowers and fruit and clothing and buildings and the deep blue of the Indian sky make the noonday sun seem brighter. The visitor's ears and eyes are filled. Both are bewildered.

After a while, when the newcomer has learned to talk with the people in one of their many languages, some of the street sounds are given rhythm and meaning. Later, too, the newcomer adjusts to the dazzling colors. The traveler has begun to feel at home in India.

9

SOUND AND COLOR

IN AMERICA we are accustomed to hearing church bells and train bells and school bells. In India there are bells everywhere. Elephants wear them, and camels and goats, and tonga horses have a jingling string on the harness across their chests. Bells are a part of Hindu worship and are rung constantly in the temples.

Another bell-like sound is the tinkling of the anklets and bracelets worn by Indian women, which make a gentle tune with every movement of arm or foot.

Indian people like to sing. They are not self-conscious and they sing at times when an American would be embarrassed. In India if a man is alone, walking along a road at night, he sings loudly. It is fine company and it keeps away the evil spirits that might molest him. In the daytime at work, the song divides whatever he is doing into parts and the time passes even though he has no one to talk to him. So any lone gardener, drawing up water from a well with only a pair of bullocks for companionship, sings the well song, a monotonous chant, repeated again and again. It has directions in it which the bullocks understand. There is a phrase for each section, a long pull and the bucket reaches the top and the song soars. The dripping bucket is overturned into the little sluice-way leading to the garden and the water rushes along it. The tune descends when the bucket or water skin is again dropped into the well.

Animals and birds are part of the daily soundtrack in India. Flocks of wild parrots scream in the fruit trees. At night, peacocks flying in to settle on a home tree near a village, utter a meowing cry which makes one think of an army of cats. There is a small, drab bird, almost never seen, but heard maddeningly in the hot weather on the Indian plains. Its mournful notes seem to say "brain-fever, brain-fever, brain-fever" over and over again throughout a long hot afternoon.

There are always the crows, gossiping busily all day long and punctuating everything that goes on, whether it is in the yard of a residence, called a compound, or on the roof of a bank, with their ceaseless "caw, caw, caw".

Then there are the hawkers, men who make a living by carrying their wares around with them because they are too poor to own a shop. They are constantly shouting their goods—fruit, pan, hot tea, especially at railroad stations.

All of these things may seem annoying at first to a stranger, but when one lives in India for any length of time they become so familiar that they are much missed when the visitor returns to his own country.

Even if one's ears are offended in the beginning in India, the eye is not. No one who has ever seen from a train window bright red chili peppers, banked up in a symmetrical mound waiting for a dealer to come and bargain can ever forget it. Above is the blue sky. Beneath is the bare earth, already dry in the warmth of late March and swept clean like a frame for the women's wares. They have patiently picked the peppers, carried them in baskets, helped to smooth them into the long rectangle for display. They will be paid for their hard work. Not enough, possibly. But they have also had something beautiful to work with.

Indian love of color goes back many centuries. The Greek historian, Megasthenes, records in his early writings about India, a little after the time of Alexander the Great, how the people were fond of bright colors in their dress and their jeweled ornaments.

There is color everywhere in the dress of the people on the street, particularly on a market day and at a country fair. The turbans of the men, sometimes denoting caste or occupation in the way they are wound, may be of any color as well as white. The wandering *sadhu*, a seeker of truth, wears a long yellow robe. A low caste woman, one who does washing, a *dhobin*, can be recognized by the pattern of the material in the full skirt she wears, in stripes of red and brown and green and yellow.

It is a lovely sight to watch an Indian woman going along a road. Her shoulders are well back, her head is high, her bare feet are sure. Her steps are rhythmic and graceful and her heels kick the hem of her skirt at the back at the spaced interval of her step like the pendulum of a clock. Long years of carrying burdens on her head, a water jar, or a bundle of washing, a basket of vegetables for market, or, if she is an outcaste woman, a basket of cowdung to make fuel cakes, have trained her to walk as gracefully as one expects a queen to move. Underneath her head scarf a heavy round pad rests on her hair to help her burden balance more securely. And though her occupation is humble, she is a woman and her veil, a red one perhaps, is worn partly across her face, in modest shyness.

Who ever heard of a little boy wearing red satin trousers? Or having a hat decorated with gilt spangles that make it look like a crown? Some little boys do wear such things in India. A few.

And who ever heard of a little girl with a bright jewel set in her nostril like an earring? Some little girls in India have their noses pierced, princesses and daughters of merchants and the ones who dance for a living.

Those things might be true, but who ever did hear of a pink palace? There is one, in India, though it sounds like a fairy tale. One has a feeling of living in a continuous fairy tale, sometimes, there, where there is so much gorgeous color everywhere. Even plain things are beautiful when one sees them colored. A common water jar made by the potter in the bazaar by the dozen and sold by him for only a few cents, is made of clay which turns a deep red when it is baked in the kiln. The potter puts a lump of dull gray clay in the center of his wheel, laid flat in front of him where he crouches on the ground. While the wheel spins he shapes the clay with his hands into a water jar or a little handleless cup or a shallow bowl. When he has enough things for the furnace he sets them in to bake and when they come out they are hard and no longer dull looking. Each piece looks better and worth more because it has acquired color.

It is only a natural thing that Indians should appreciate color and use it lavishly. They see it in Nature, in flowers and trees, some of which are in bloom in some part of India the year round, and in the gifts of the earth. The richest precious stones of the whole world have come from India. Much of this kind of wealth is buried away in huge treasure rooms, securely guarded. But a great deal of it is worn on state occasions by Indian royalty. Even their elephants are gaily dressed then, in jeweled velvet saddle cloths, and bright designs are painted on their leathery old hides. A mahout's white teeth shine in his dark face and his eyes flash with pride in his animal when they move into position, carrying a prince perhaps in the gilded howdah high on the elephant's back for all the people to see.

The pink palace is in Jaipur, one of the Princely States of the Rajputana Federation. The state colors of Jaipur are pink and gold, a deep orange gold. By order of the prince who was reigning in 1728 and who began the building of the modern capital, all the buildings of Jaipur City are pink. They have tinted plaster walls or are made of the rose-pink sandstone of which the old Moghuls made such glorious use in their heyday. The Rajah's bodyguard wears a white uniform, with glittering black-polished leather boots and blue and white striped turbans. It may not be a coincidence that one variety of the oleander shrub has pink blossoms and that it grows happily in the acrid soil of Rajputana.

The gods in the temples are gilded and painted with rich color. The deep orange of marigold blossoms is seen everywhere, almost a sacred flower of the Hindus because it is used so much by worshippers. Sometimes a single blossom is laid on a small wayside shrine. Usually someone takes the trouble to see that even such an unimportant spot is cleaned and freshened and made ready for the new season when everything in Hinduism is whitewashed and decorated at the feast of Diwali.

The plaster walls of shops and houses, and even drab mud walls, offer pleasant possibilities to Indian artists. Gay figures of Ganesh, the elephant god, much beloved all over Hindustan, birds, or some symbol dear to the family in the house will appear in rude colors made from home dyes if the women have time. They have no money to buy framed pictures for their walls inside, so they draw them on the outside, with Nature and religious symbols for their models. A sense of all artistic ways is born deep in every Indian and they express it unselfconsciously.

Taste and touch are associated with color in India to a greater degree than they are in America. Cocoanut, appearing on New York pushcarts in season, white against the thick brown husk, brings again to the tongue the taste of a fish curry, the way they do it in South India, with a golden gravy and shreds of the fresh nut hidden in it. It does, if one has eaten that curry, ever. Perhaps smell has a part in color, too. A bruised chrysanthemum leaf in an American florist's shop can bring to mind the memory of rows and rows of white ones, in pots, edging the veranda and drive of a modest house in North India. It can, if one has lived in that house and touched those plants.

Saffron is used to flavor and color a dessert of rice and raisins called *halwa.* The thick gravy of a cooked legume called *dal,* somewhat like dried peas in the United States, is sometimes a golden yellow and sometimes a deep, sage green, according to the variety used.

A heaping plate of rice, covered with dal, and a ripe mango make a fine meal. The pink sections of a pomelo, something like our American grapefruit, sprinkled with shredded cocoanut is a favorite dessert in North India where the best pomelo grow.

Without any doubt the most gorgeous color gathered in any one place is in the tail feathers of the peacock, the male of the pea fowl. The hen is dull beside him. The great fan of his tail spreads in an enormous arc of shimmering blue and green and bronze and at the tip of each is an eye shape made by the shaded colorings. This bird is sacred among the Hindus. There are many flocks all over India. Farmers find they are destructive in their grain fields, but the Hindu law of life protects them. It is an offense in civil law to send peacock feathers out of the country.

The people of India, the sounds they make and the colors they use and wear, make their country a special place to dwell in, to remember and to love.

Bill Witt from Black Star

The tomb of Prince Humayun, father of the more famous Akbar, near New Delhi, built of red sandstone and white marble. This is one of the Moghuls' earliest buildings.

A night school which adults may attend, part of the adult education project in United Provinces.

Press Information Bureau, Government of India

The public letter-writer and two customers. These men are Muslims. The pens are sharpened pieces of bamboo.

Deane Dickason from Ewing Galloway, N. Y.

Harry Lewis from Black Star

A Jain temple and garden. In the lamp pillar at the left there is fine detail of the colored inlaid work much used by the Jains in decoration.

Berko from Black Star

A worshipper in the act of prayer at a temple in Bombay. Notice the bell and the lotus carvings on the pillars.

An Indian village scene. Notice the structure of the houses and the bullock cart.

Bill Witt from Black Star

The double-decked camel cart is still in use in some parts of India. Bundles and produce go below, people above.

Bill Witt from Black Star

Harry Lewis from Black Star

Low caste village woman (Hindu) taking finished dung cakes from a wall where they have been spread to dry. These are used for cooking fuel.

Hindus bathing in the Ganges River at Hardwar, a place of special pilgrimage, during a religious festival.

Nanja Nath from Black Star

Sam B. Tata from Black Star

South Indian washerwomen. The stones on the river bank are used for washboards. Across the stream is a temple.

Press Information Bureau, Government of India

The wheel, Buddhist symbol of life as a perfect circle, appears frequently in Hindu architecture in the period after many Buddhist teachings were absorbed into the Hindu religion. This one is in the Temple of the Sun at Konarak, Orissa.

UNATIONS from Black Star

Rice is a staple food all over India. To improve the yield and its quality a commission has been set up in the Province of Orissa much like Agricultural Experiment stations in the United States. Rice is still husked by hand or by bullocks trampling the straw on a threshing floor.

UNATIONS from Black Star

Deane Dickason from Ewing Galloway, N. Y.

A modern steel and iron works mill near Mysore in South India.

Berko from Black Star

Child of a cultured family in an art school. He is a Hindu.

Bill Witt from Black Star

Hindu girl with pierced nostril. The ring keeps the hole open so that a jewel may be inserted when she is older.

Nanja Nath from Black Star

Modern methods and equipment are making India schools more attractive for children than those attended by their parents or even their older brothers and sisters.

Small Muslim boys at an outdoor school session. Their slates are wood, painted black.

Déane Dickason from Ewing Galloway, N. Y.

Harry Lewis from Black Star

Muslim women wearing the protective boorkah, which they must wear in public. This practice is slowly dying out.

Deane Dickason from Ewing Galloway, N. Y.

One of the patient workers in carved ivory in Old Delhi. It takes several years to make the sort of piece he holds.

A scene in the upper Sind valley, through which early Aryans came down into India. This Himalayan peak is about 16,000 feet.

Deane Dickason from Ewing Galloway, N. Y.

The famous Khyber Pass. Over its barren roads enemy invaders and peaceful caravans have entered India for centuries.

Ewing Galloway, N. Y.

IV. RELIGION

THE ancient faiths of India penetrate to every part of the people's lives, whether they worship the God of the Muslim or the Christian, or Brahma, the Creative Force of the Hindus.

The temple or the mosque is the heart of an Indian village. The call to worship from the mosque is part of the voice of the multitude in an Indian street. The sacred tulsi plant brings Brahma into the humblest Indian home. Palaces have their private chapels.

Buddhist priests still tend the shrine in Gaya or search India's roads for the way of escape from the Wheel of Life, and Hindu holy men measure their length in the dust to appease the wrath of the gods whom they go to worship in Benares, their sacred city.

Every Thursday night at sundown little lamps are lighted all over India at Muslim tombs. In dignified vaults or on isolated graves along the roadsides, some faithful follower of the Prophet devotedly places the small saucer of oil with its cotton wick, because Friday is their holy day and by so doing he gains some merit for himself.

On Sundays the Christians fill their cathedrals and churches and small houses of worship in country villages.

God is everywhere in India.

10

THE ANCIENT FAITHS OF INDIA

THE MANY unique aspects of her ancient faiths have set India apart among the nations and it is necessary, in order to understand her slow political development, to know something about the various religious teachings. The most significant fact about the religions of India is neither age, nor origin nor type of teachings, but, taken together, the conflicts which have been aroused between the respective followers of Hinduism and Islam and the manner in which each faith has become a political division.

Each group is spoken of as a *community*, in the sense that each member has a feeling of loyalty to his particular religion in common with other worshippers of the same faith. In America our usual use of that word is to denote a town or a village or a small group of farms, but the Indian usage must be kept in mind to follow the story. *Communalism*, then, in India is religious plus political loyalty. Indians have not yet, generally, been able to grasp the meaning of their new statehood. If one is asked his nationality he is much more apt to say that he is a Hindu, or a Christian or a Muslim rather than that he is an Indian.

Contrary to political custom in other countries it is not possible for a minority party in one election to become the party in power in the next. The Hindus have the largest population. Therefore, they can decide favorably to themselves any election. Knowing that they would always be in the minority, the Muslims preferred to set up their own state in 1947 rather than risk not receiving the safeguards they had earlier argued for in all proposed plans for becoming a free India. Indians at this point were Hindu and Muslim first and Indian second. Until the idea of having two separate states was accepted, the question of safeguards demanded by the Muslims delayed and hindered any accomplishment. It was not, as many people believed, Great Britain's reluctance to let India establish its own government, which caused the delay. It was the way it was to be done which could not be easily decided.

Buddhism is important in a study of the religions of India because of its influence upon early Hinduism.

Many of its teachings were adopted by the Hindu priests and taken over when Hinduism enjoyed a great revival and Buddhism began to die away.

The founder was an Indian prince named Siddhartha. At his birth there had been a prophecy made by the Hindu priests. They said: "This child will be monarch of all the world if he abides in a household. But if he should retire from the worldly life he will become a Buddha—a Wise One—and will find a way to ease the world of sin and folly."

His father, the Rajah Suddhodana, wanted to know how it would come about, if his son should ever decide to leave the normal life of a household. He was told that whenever the young prince should see an old man, a sick man, a dead man and a holy man, then he would renounce the world. The king, like all fathers, thought he knew what was best for his son and he determined that the youth should never look upon the four kinds of men who would change his life. So the prince was protected from unpleasant things of all kinds. He was surrounded by friends and attendants of his own age so that he might not be reminded that people grow old. The gardeners in the king's estates were careful that he should never see even one withered blossom or dead leaf on the plants, so that he would never think of death. No holy men were allowed inside the palaces and the gardens where the prince passed his life.

So he grew to manhood and was married to a beautiful princess. In time they had a baby son. But he was growing restless in his garden prison and one day he asked for his horse and his royal carriage and his driver and he went outside to the king's park. On his journey he saw some strange people. One was a bent old man walking with the help of a stick. Another was a man being carried by his friends because he was so wasted with disease that he could no longer walk; a little farther on, he saw a corpse being prepared for its funeral pyre; and last of all he saw a man with an expression on his face such as he had never seen on any other in the whole world, not even on his father's. That man looked as if he had peace.

Siddartha had many questions to ask, for he had never seen such strange sights before and so it fell that his driver, a humble man, became his teacher and he found that day that it is every person's lot to follow the cycle of life—birth, youth, young manhood, middle age, old age and death. None escape. It is appointed.

Surely there must be some way out of such a fate. Siddartha resolved to find it. He was fulfilling the prophecy. He renounced the world so that he might find peace for himself and all mankind. The story of his wanderings in his search for enlightenment is written in the holy books of the Buddhists, for this was the prince who became Gautama Buddha and received enlightenment under a green bo tree in Gaya, in the kingdom of Orissa.

The Buddhists believe that the wheel is the one perfect form in the universe and that all of life is a

Wheel of Law, to which mortals are bound and from which only their own conduct will release them. Buddha taught that self-control, kindness to others and reverence for all life, even in the lowliest creatures, was necessary to achieve deliverance from the Wheel, and to find everlasting peace when one has at last given up all desire for material things.

Gautama Buddha established a new religious order with his teachings. His disciples went all over India, preaching in the popular language of the people, Prakit. His teachers were known as monks, and monasteries were established in many places.

The beliefs of Buddhism were in sharp contrast to the unwieldy laws of the Hindu priests and the many demands of the caste system which even in those early days were beginning to bind the people more and more rigidly. So there were many converts to the new faith. It aroused the Brahman priests and brought about in time a great Hindu revival. It is notable that the modern Hindu religion embodies many Buddhistic teachings. Hindus even like to claim that Buddha was one of the manifestations of their god Vishnu on earth.

Buddhism was strong and was not entirely destroyed until the Muslims came in the thirteenth century and burned the monasteries and killed the monks.

Everything in Buddhism and Hinduism is directly opposed to the principles of the Muslim. He abhors the worship of idols and teaches that all men are equal. The faith of Islam is democratic. The Hindu caste system is aristocratic. It was inevitable that the two should clash.

The Muslim religion is anti-Christian in that, while they do worship one god, it is Mohammed as his Prophet whom they respect and revere. They refuse to recognize Christ as superior in any way.

The Hindu religion is non-Christian. They worship one god as a creative force in the world, but they recognize thousands of gods which each represent some one part of that force.

The Muslim kills cows for food. To the Hindu the cow is the representative of the Mother Spirit. The first chapattie baked at the morning hearth-fire is given to the family cow. Bulls with two humps are especially sacred and are allowed to wander in town or village at their will, with no work, and the choice of the bazaar stalls for food. If a stall owner drives an animal away, it is at his own risk of the gods' anger.

The Muslim worships quietly, kneeling to pray at morning and noon and dusk, with his face turned to the east, when the call of the muezzin, the public crier, is heard from his high tower in the mosque. That call is one of the distinctive sounds of India, threading through all the other noises of traffic and talk and work, three times a day. "Allah is Great and Mohammed is His Prophet", high and clear the chant floats, almost like that of a cantor in a Jewish temple in America.

The Muslim prays with his face turned to the east, because Mecca is there, the sacred city of the Prophet.

That word, too, we have absorbed into our American speech. To us, Mecca means a goal or an objective, the expression of a great desire. Every Muslim wants to make the pilgrimage to Mecca some day. Those who have made it are known always thereafter by their beards, dyed red.

The Hindu is noisy in his worship. Whether in his temple or a religious procession, he shouts and sings and lets all the world know that he is giving homage to his gods. The shrine in the temple is hung about with bells which the worshipper rings to attract the attention of the god. There are groups of religious drummers attached to some temples and the fire worship at Muttra on the bank of the Jumna River, one of the sacred cities of the Northern Hindus, is accompanied with a fine ritual of bell ringing. A peculiarly penetrating sound, like that of a deep-toned horn, is made by blowing on conch shells.

It is easy to see why a Muslim would be irritated when interrupted in his quiet act of prayer by a noisy Hindu procession passing the mosque, with a full accompaniment of conch shell music.

Once in Lucknow, the capital of the province of Uttar Pradesh in North India, that very thing did happen, and the angry Muslims rose up off their prayer rugs and ran for the nearest bricks to throw at the offenders. The riot which then took place kept the whole city in turmoil for a week. Frightened Muslim and Hindu women, who had never gone out on the streets alone, were marooned and hungry in their own houses because their men stayed away to fight or had been killed. Many of the women were rescued by friendly European residents of the city who offered their services to the district police.

The strange part of this ancient enmity between the religions is that there are friendships between individual Hindus and Muslims. On the staff of any European household the cook may be a Muslim and the table man a Hindu and other servants of the casteless untouchables, yet all are friendly and join together in the family prayers which their mistress often likes to conduct among them.

Muslims do not observe caste, but they keep their womenfolk strictly secluded, not allowing them to go about freely in public, and when they must make journeys, requiring them to wear the stifling *burqa*, a clumsy, enveloping garment which covers a woman from head to foot, with small peepholes for her eyes. It is a wonderful disguise, too, and is often used by escaping criminals. This has retarded social growth in India. If women can hear and see only what goes on in their own households their minds are not stimulated to learn.

The wearing of the burqa will some day die out, because young Indian women are rebelling against it. Many of them are being sent to European schools because the fathers have realized that girl children have good minds if they have an opportunity to use them.

A number of years ago a Muslim girl attempted to wear a burqa and yet attend college. It was her family's idea, not hers. She wore a large straw sailor hat of obvious western manufacture and gathered around its crown were the wide folds of the enveloping muslin garment. The poor girl looked like a moving tent. It was a girls' college so the only men who might see her face, if it was not covered, were the servants about the place. The girl stood it a while and then emerged from her cotton prison to mingle more freely with her college mates and to be seen occasionally by some humble gardener or the office boy. It took courage and it scandalized her family, but they had to accept it as one of the by-products of the good education they wanted her to have.

Caste may have been a help in organizing the Hindus in the early days. It has been only a hindrance in later times. The system is the oldest and one of the most significant reasons for the long delay in the growth of Indian national feeling and pride; why India, though so old, is one of the newest nations. The various levels of society, strictly marked, kept the Hindus so separated that they were unable to think of themselves as being Indians first and together, no matter what their caste might be.

Caste law demands strict observance of many tiresome details of living. These, combined with religious ritual, make the orthodox Hindu's day very complicated. It is strange and wonderful that India has been able to become so great when independent thought had so little room to grow in for hundreds of years. All of a man's thinking had been done for him long before.

Caste ruled that:

A child could not play with another child unless they were of the same caste.

A caste person could not partake of food cooked by a person of another caste.

A caste person might not marry a person of another caste.

If the shadow of a lower caste person or an outcaste person should fall upon food while a caste man was eating, the food was considered defiled and must be thrown away.

Many times innocent people suffered for such a supposed sin. There were so many requirements and forbidden things, so much ceremonial in connection with the preparation and eating of food, built up by degrees by the priests, that it became impossible for men to travel far from home without breaking caste. This retarded travel overseas and international association and as a consequence it affected the growth of national feeling. The ritual of reinstatement in caste, once it had been broken, was difficult to experience.

The Jains are Hindus. Their teachings are similar to those of Buddhism and the sect was established at about the same time. Their chief distinction from orthodox Hinduism is the emphasis they place on obedience to the law, "Thou shalt not kill". Many wear small white masks over their mouths and noses so as not to breathe in, unknowingly, some small insect and cause its death. Others carry small brooms and sweep the ground in front of them as they walk so that they will not tread on anything that crawls and hurt it. The last of the Jain kings, so an old story goes, was defeated because he refused to send his army on a march on a rainy night, when he could have taken his enemy unaware, because of the insects they would destroy by stepping on them in the dark.

They are strict vegetarians, though they even believe that plants have souls. Because of their extreme efforts not to take life they are limited in their economic and professional activities. They may not be soldiers. They may not be farmers, for a plough might crush a mole or a worm. They may not be doctors or nurses. Yet they are usually well-to-do because all their intelligence has been bent to business.

The temples of the Jains are beautiful. A noted one is in Calcutta, a sparkling small edifice which glitters with bits of mirror and bright mosaics set in the walls. There are many shelters for wounded animals supported by Jain money and patronage.

Still another sect of the Hindus is the group of fierce-looking bearded men of the Punjab, called Sikhs, who have provided the Indian Army with many brave officers and fighting men and in times past served the British as international police in China and Japan.

Originally the Sikhs were not aggressive. Their leader, Nanak, set down in a book called the *Granth* all of his ideas for reform in Hinduism. He felt that the worship of idols had developed into an evil thing, and that the caste system covered many wrongs. He preached against both idol worship and caste and won many followers to agree with him. They adopted Nanak's ideas as their religious principles, but they were not bigoted in their new-found faith. They intended tolerance toward all religions.

Akbar, the famous Moghul Emperor, came to the throne in 1556, over fifteen years after the death of Nanak, the Sikh leader, but he became interested and gave the new organization the land upon which they later built their Golden Temple in Amritsar. In it they placed their sacred book, the *Granth*, under a rich canopy. Worshipful Sikhs bow before it, lay their offerings there and bring votive flowers, and by so doing have merely exchanged one form of image worship for another.

It was only in later years, when the Sikhs were obliged to defend themselves against Akbar's successors, that they developed into the modern fierce fighter. They observe absolute equality and brotherhood. It is part of their religious requirement that the hair is worn long and knotted on top of the head under a spruce, fine fitting turban. The daily routine of dressing beard and hair and arranging the turban takes a great deal of time. Those who observe all the forms and ceremonies religiously, as ordered by the *Granth*, may assume the name Singh, meaning Lion, though not all with that name in India are Sikhs.

Many missionaries of both Catholic and Protestant faiths have worked in India for years. Christianity offered to the untouchables and to the lower castes within Hinduism a way out of their hard lot in life and they flocked to the missions. Many fine schools and hospitals have been built and the Christians are now large enough in numbers to be reckoned as one of the distinct communities in political representation in the new government.

The Syrian Christians set up their church in South India two thousand years ago. Tradition says that Thomas, the Doubter, lived among them. They keep a light burning above a grave in St. Thomas Cathedral in Madras which is reputed to be his.

These—the Hindu, the Muslim, the Buddhist, the Jain, the Sikh and the Christian—are the principal religious faiths in India.

11

FOLKLORE AND SUPERSTITIONS

THE LARGER PERCENTAGE of India's people live in country villages far away from cities. They work very hard and few have had time to go to school. It is quite natural, because of this, that they should be extremely superstitious, fearing everything which they do not understand. Though they are counted as Hindus, their religion means little more than a life-long attempt to appease gods and demons who may harm them. They fear the works of both, but more than all they fear ghosts which they call *bhuts*.

In order not to offend some god they may not know about, they assume there is a god for everything, even for contagious diseases. The priests in the village temples encourage this, because they are able to do a flourishing business in the sale of amulets. These are charms to frighten away every known evil which may threaten the life of mankind. The people buy them for preventing evil and for bringing good. They are worn round their necks so that the god will see and be pleased.

The strings of large blue beads round the necks of oxen are put there to avoid the Evil Eye. That is the first and accepted purpose of beads, from ancient times, more for a charm than a decoration.

According to the Laws of Manu, one of the ancient Hindu books, a baby boy's tongue must be touched with honey and butter at birth. The father performs this ceremony and repeats the ceremonial words: "O long-lived one, mayst thou live a hundred years in this world, protected by the gods". He touches the baby's shoulder and pronounces this blessing: "Become firm as a rock, sharp as an axe, pure as gold; thou art called a son; live thou a hundred years".

It is believed by merchants that the first customer of the morning will bring him good luck if the person buys something. Therefore, the first shopper to appear is very likely to get an extremely good bargain, particularly if he shows signs of indifference to the wares.

Trees are supposed to be inhabited by unseen spirits, the enemies of travelers. A villager dislikes walking along a road at night alone, even when the moon is high, because of his fears, and he will sing lustily, in the hope of driving the spirits away. Sometimes the singing is very good.

When long journeys are planned by a family, either by cart or train, they must consult the village priest to find an auspicious day. The priest casts a horoscope, with the traveler's plans in mind. Sometimes the priest is not consulted and the villager depends upon some simple sign of Nature for his guidance, particularly if he does not have the money to pay at the temple for such help.

Even dacoits, the robber bands who roam India, robbing villagers of their precious silver hoarded against tax day or rent day, will wait upon some kind of sign for the right day to carry out their next theft. One way they do it is to take a handful of wheat and divide it, grain by grain, into piles of four. If it comes out even, that is not the day. If one grain only is left over, then that might be a good time to go.

In South India, there is a cult of snake worshippers who believe that members of a household will never want for anything if snakes are allowed to live in the house. The snake is looked upon as one of the incarnations of god. In some homes in Malabar one room is left for the use of the snakes. Milk is provided for them to drink and not one member of the family would think of molesting any snake that chose to nest in that room, for fear of the gods' anger.

The origin of the snake cult is an ancient Hindu legend. A cobra once defended Brahma, the Creator, from the sun while he lay asleep, by spreading its hood for shade. There is a mark, resembling a face, on the back of cobras' hoods which the people believe was put there by Brahma in gratitude.

A common description of an elephant is "the animal with a snake between its eyes", and when an elephant is painted and decorated for a procession the mark at the top of the trunk looks something like a cobra's hood.

Early in August in North India there is a special day when serpents are worshipped and are offered milk to drink. When they have consumed it all, the snakes are then supposed to hibernate throughout the cold weather.

While tigers are not worshipped, the Indian people have a great deal of respect for this lord of the jungle even when a man-eater has killed a number of people from one village. They have developed some strange beliefs connected with this animal. Oil made from tiger fat is supposed to have healing properties for rheumatism. When a tiger is killed on a shoot, there is rivalry among the men for the lucky bones, which are found at the point of the shoulder. Special good fortune is supposed to come to anyone carrying these bones about on his person.

European hunters who wish to have a fine tiger skin as a trophy of a hunt have to take special precautions for getting the whiskers intact, because their Indian helpers prize them for the magic qualities they are said to possess. A necklace of tiger claws is supposed to give great strength to the wearer. And if a piece of dried tiger flesh is hung round a baby's neck, the child will be protected from all wild beasts.

There are other superstitions connected with teeth. One is that if a little baby who is cutting teeth is made to wear a necklace of fish teeth, his own will be stronger.

Every nation has its wise sayings and proverbs, which differ only in the way they are said. Probably the origin of some of them goes back to the days of King Solomon. In India, one can imagine the old men of a small village sitting under the council tree in the evening, smoking, and talking over different people they know, using words and names of objects familiar to all to express their thoughts. The sayings would go something like this:

The young of a cuckoo will after all be a cuckoo.

The hubble-bubble (a water pipe that men smoke) in the hands of a monkey.

Music hath no charms for a buffalo.

To the blind day and night are the same.

Like the tusk and teeth of an elephant, one set for show and another to eat with.

The voice of a boaster is like the breeze of a fan pitted against the hurricane.

He was born but yesterday and today he is a giant.

Useless desire is like an earless woman wishing for earrings.

A dog is brave at his own door.

There are many legends about the Hindu gods, some of whom are believed to have come to earth in human form at times to aid mankind. Rama was one of these. He is thought to have been one of the ancient kings of Oudh which is now a part of the province of Uttar Pradesh. He was skilled at archery and was the only prince who was able to lift or bend the mighty bow of King Janaka.

The god Krishna is most often represented with a flute, symbolizing the call of god to men.

Ganesh, the god with the elephant head, is probably the most grotesquely shaped of the god images, unless it be Kali with her many arms. Ganesh is well beloved, however, while Kali is feared. He has a jolly, plump little figure, and rides on a rat.

When Ganesh was born to Durga, the wife of Shiva the Destroyer, he was a beautiful child. An envious, evil spirit caused his head to drop off. His mother wept and his father promised her that he would bring in the head of the first living creature he met. That was an elephant and its head was given to the little boy. To make up for his ugly fate he was made the god of success. Everyone who begins a new enterprise offers a sacrifice to Ganesh. He is worshipped just before a wedding so that the long ceremony will go smoothly.

He gets more attention than many of the other gods because the people want him to smile on their projects. In some communities Ganesh is worshipped as god of the harvest, because he rides a rat, and thereby controls them so that they leave the grain alone.

The red brahminy kite, a bird of South India, is identified with the strange eagle figure upon which Vishnu the Preserver rides. It is considered very lucky and a sign of good omen if one should see this bird on a Thursday or a Sunday.

In South India, too, where cocoanut trees abound, it is the custom to break a cocoanut on the occasion of commencing a new piece of business. The god Shiva is the patron of the cocoanut, because he has three eyes as it does.

Indian superstition extends to its songs. There are special ones for particular times of day and no song is ever sung out of order or turn. There is a Frog Hymn in the *Rig-Veda*, an ancient sacred book. It is believed that the frog influences the coming of rain.

There is a great deal of superstition about the moon, particularly in North India. If any person sees the new moon in the Hindu month *Bhadon*, which is our months of August and September, he is sure to be accused of some sin, falsely, during the coming year. When he does see the new moon accidentally, the result can be avoided if a friend can be persuaded to throw a few bricks at his house. A peculiar tabu about food is connected with the moon. No one is supposed to eat cooked food for eight hours after an eclipse.

It is difficult to understand how the rural people of India can be happy when they have such a hard life, a life so full of do's and don'ts in every daily act, and so full of fear when something is forgotten or disobeyed. The answer is that there is usually a penance one may do to avoid the penalty of one's acts, and there is always plenty of miserable company in one's village if the penalty persists.

Nowadays the village people are learning slowly to read for themselves, the men and the women, and it will not take them long to find out that much they have feared all their lives can do them no harm.

12

THE LEGEND OF RAMA AND SITA

MANY STORIES have been known so long in India that no one can say when they were first told. Such a one is *The Ramayana*, an epic poem many thousands of lines long. Not many people could read in ancient days in India and so the tales of old battles and gods and heroes were told to children by their parents and grandparents, who had learned them in the same way. Minstrels sang the stories in royal courts. In the bazaars men told each other the tales in the poem for amusement while they waited for customers.

Such was the manner in which the story of the great Prince Rama was learned by the people of India. Probably in the many tellings some things were added which were not a part of the original story. But the man in Bengal knows it in the speech of his Province, Bengali. The children in North India know it in Hindi. Yet it was originally told and later written down in Sanskrit, the early language of the Hindus. In English it still keeps its ancient theme, a story of adventure and exciting rescues, of battles with demons and other evil spirits, of mythical animals and great inventions, of loyalty and bravery, of enduring friendships and the victory of all things good.

Here is a short and very free translation of the best loved of all the stories in *The Ramayana*, the legend of Rama and his wife Sita, who was a beautiful princess.

Once upon a time, and that was very long ago, there lived a brave young Prince and his name was Rama. He had great strength and was so kind to animals that they wanted to do what he said. He could also understand their speech. The people of his father's kingdom, Ayodhya, liked him more than any of his three brothers. Some of the people believed that he was the god Vishnu the Preserver, come to earth in human form.

Rama and his brothers were trained, as all princes are, to be strong of mind and body and to excel if possible in all things. And so Rama and the other princes learned to shoot with arrows from a bow and always hit the mark. They learned how to wrestle, how to make music, how to repeat the classics, and how to reason in philosophy.

Also, Rama learned to be patient and modest before his superiors, and was gifted with a good memory which helped him many times in his life.

One day when he was sixteen years old, a great adventure befell. That day started like any other day with his morning duties and lessons. Then he and his brother Lakshmana were summoned to the court. They found a visitor there, a saintly king who had come on a long journey to ask for help. He wanted the two princes to return with him and get rid of some wicked demons which were besetting his kingdom. The boys' strength and bravery were well known and the visitor was sure they could do what he wished.

Rama and Lakshmana immediately said they would go, though their father was anxious as most fathers would be, about letting them risk any danger.

They made the return journey with the saintly king and when they arrived at the end of it the evil spirits appeared. The sky grew black, the wind blew, and the demons howled but Rama and his brother slew them all. The news went out to the Lord of Demons himself, Ravana, in his stronghold in Lanka, which is now the Island of Ceylon, that a new enemy, much to be feared, had appeared in the North.

The old king was very grateful and invited the princes to stay for a visit but they said if there was nothing more to do, they ought to be going home. Before they went their host thought they would like to see the mighty bow which was the possession of his neighbor, King Janaka. No prince had yet come who could even move it, much less bend it. The king had said that the hand of his daughter Sita would be given to the prince who could bend the bow.

So the two princes consented to go and see it. It was indeed a mighty bow. It was so large that it had to be carried on a huge cart drawn by many bullocks. No one had ever been able to lift it off the cart.

Rama lifted the bow easily and bent it in his two hands. There was a great shout from the crowd which had gathered to watch. Then he fitted an arrow and shot it and it went so far that it was not found that day nor the next. But the people believed that in the place where it fell a mighty river of pure water sprang out of the ground.

There was feasting and laughter at the court afterward, and the marriage of Rama and Sita was arranged. He was a very fortunate prince for she was a beautiful princess and they were very happy.

When Rama returned home with his bride, his father was pleased and decided to bestow upon him part of the ruling power. But Rama was not the favorite son of the queen. Her favorite was named Bharata. Just before the king was ready to carry out his plan, the queen, who had once saved her husband's life, claimed the two wishes he had promised her at that time. One wish was that Bharata be given the honored place instead of Rama. The other was that Rama be exiled to the forest for fourteen years.

Rama's father, the king, did not know what to do. He did not want Bharata's help in ruling the kingdom. He did not want to send Rama, his beloved son, to the life of a forest dweller. But he had promised the queen that she could have two wishes for saving his life. What could he do?

Then Rama, perceiving the trouble in his father's mind, insisted that there was only one thing to do, and that was to grant the queen her wishes. So, reluctantly, the king gave to Bharata, the queen's favorite son, the place of honor that was to have been Rama's. Then Rama and Sita, and Lakshmana with them, went to the forest to live. The king was very sad and he and many of the loyal subjects made part of the journey to the forest with the three, in farewell for fourteen years.

Rama and Sita thought they would have a long life of joy and simple pleasure, with the animals and the beautiful forest flowers all round them. But Rama's fame as a strong man with the bow followed him to the forest.

His father died and his brother, the queen's favorite, did not wish to rule. He came to the forest to beg Rama to return. But Rama, taking off his sandals, gave them to his brother and thereby renounced for a time his claim to the throne. His brother went home and set the golden sandals on the throne itself, and ruled for Rama.

While living in the forest Rama again conquered and slew some fierce demons who had been terrorizing the people. The demons were ugly to look at, with wings like bats and hairy faces. Another message went faster than the winds of heaven to Ravana in his island palace. He was very angry and flew north to avenge the deaths of his followers.

Now demons have the power to take different forms, more pleasing than their own. And they had by tricks and maneuvers threatened the life of the beautiful Sita. Rama and Lakshmana did not like to leave her alone because of this, and yet they were obliged to often, when going to battle, or hunting for their food. Then the King of the Vultures, a great bird, volunteered to carry her on his back and always watch over the princess whenever the brothers had to be away.

But when Ravana, Lord of all the Demons, came he was more powerful than the great bird and stole Sita away to his kingdom in the South, leaving the King of the Vultures dying on a lonely hillside.

Sita had no way to leave a message so she dropped some of her jewels while Ravana was flying away with her, and they fell on the Monkey Mountains.

When Rama returned and discovered the dying vulture he found out what had happened. When they had made a funeral pyre and had burned the body of the loyal bird, they set out for the South to find Sita—Rama and Lakshmana together—and came in time to the Monkey Mountains. They found the chief of the monkeys in great need of help in battle with his brother who had seized his kingdom. So Rama made a bargain that they would help the monkeys if the monkeys would help find Sita in return.

Rama's strength was again powerful enough to win a victory and when the monkey chief was restored to his own kingdom, he organized four monkey armies and sent them North and West and East and South, after telling them Rama's story, commanding that they search and not return until they had given up every hope of finding the Princess Sita.

Now the Wind God had a son called Hanuman and he was a monkey. And because he was a child of the Wind he could travel faster than any other monkey and he was sent to the South. But when he and his followers reached the sea and had not found Sita they did not know what to do. They sat down to rest and talk over their problem. If the Lord of the Demons had indeed taken Sita to the island, how would they reach it? Not even the largest, strongest monkey could leap that far.

Hanuman growled at this, made a great leap and tried to jump over the ocean. The sea demons rose up out of the water and got in his way. Monsters appeared to help them. But Hanuman defied them all and landed bravely on the island outside the palace of Ravana.

No one was about. He cautiously peeped into all the windows. He went inside and climbed the stairs. He looked in every room. In one, the great Ravana himself with his ten heads and twenty hands, lay asleep in bed. Hanuman closed that door quickly.

Sita was nowhere in the demon's palace. Hanuman was very sad. He even looked in the dungeons. Surely if she were being kept a prisoner she would be there. But no, she was not in a prison cell.

Hanuman went out into the garden and climbed a tree where he could sit and think about his trouble. He was used to thinking in trees. It might help. And then he saw the princess. She was in a little house within a wood a short distance away. But she was guarded by many ugly she-demons with thick hairy lips and horrible faces. They were asleep lying all round the lovely princess who was wide-awake but looking very sad. As sad as Hanuman felt. He was afraid to call to her for fear he would wake her keepers, but he wanted to show her the ring which Rama had given him, so that she would know he was Rama's messenger.

He began to chatter, softly, the way monkeys do when they are disturbed about anything, and Sita looked up and saw only a monkey in a tree. Then she saw the ring in his paw. Also Rama had taught her to love all animals and to understand them, so she realized after a while what the monkey was trying to say. He was begging her to ride on his back over the sea and thus be taken back to Rama.

But Sita was afraid she could not hold on tightly and that she would fall into the water, because Hanuman had no saddle or harness. Instead, she gave Hanuman the one jewel she still had, which she had been wearing in her hair, and bade him tell Rama to come with an army and conquer the Lord of the Demons and take her away.

Rama wept when Hanuman returned with his news. Then they prepared a great feast, to celebrate the fact that Sita was found and also to eat enough to grow strong for the coming battle.

Meantime the Lord of the Demons had been telling Sita a great many lies about her husband. By magic he even showed her what looked like Rama's head on a tray. But Sita knew that one day Rama would come and conquer the island demons and that good would return to the earth.

Fire and earthquakes and thunder were used to frighten the demons. Magic arrows were shot from Rama's great bow, and still the battle went on. Many monkey soldiers died. Then Rama and Lakshmana were taken prisoner and tied with ropes of living serpents.

After that Garuda, the giant bird like an eagle, on whose back Vishnu the Preserver rides, flew down to the battlefield beside the two princes. The serpents unwound themselves and crawled away in a hurry because they feared Garuda whose food is snakes.

When the monkey armies saw Rama and Lakshmana freed they renewed the battle until only a few demons were left. The fighting was fierce and lasted a long time. And none of them knew what was happening to Sita.

But at last Ravana and Rama came face to face. Rama had one more arrow, a sacred one, fitted with wings and only to be used for the best purpose. It flew straight to the heart of the ugly demon and killed him and then it bounded back and fell at Rama's feet to be used again. He picked it up, put it back in his quiver, and hurried to find Sita, his beautiful princess.

Sita was safe in the little house in the wood and all the gods rejoiced that the power of the demons was broken forever. After Sita had been purified by the rite of the Fire Ordeal because she had lived so long with the demons, she and Rama crossed back to India together.

To this day, night watchmen in India may be heard chanting "Ram, Ram, Sita, Ram" as a magic spell to keep evil spirits away from the houses they are guarding while the owners sleep.

This is only one of the many stories in *The Ramayana*. From the poem scholars have learned a great deal about the customs and beliefs of the people in the far-off times when it was first written down. We owe a great deal of thanks to the unknown Indian poet who gathered its mighty words together and preserved them for us.

13

FEASTS, FAIRS AND FUN

LIFE IN INDIA may seem very dull at times, full of hard work and bad weather. But there are so many holidays and feast days that even the poorest people have fun celebrating them. And the children have the best time of all, for the observance is usually enjoyed by the whole family together.

Practically all Indian holidays are religious in origin. Since religious custom dictates and orders everything in the Hindu way of life it is only natural that this should be true. It is the same with the Muslims. Though the Hindu worships many gods, he believes they are all a part of one God-Head. The Muslim worships one Supreme Being, and reveres one representative, Mohammed, who was his Prophet. Hindu festivals are held in honor of a particular god and Muslim ones celebrate events which were important in their religious history.

There is scarcely a time of the year in India when in some place or another the beat of drums which means a procession, or the sound of cymbals and a religious chant may not be heard. Sometimes it is only an honor for a local god, or it may be a wedding procession, escorting the groom to the bride's house. But even though such an occasion is only for a few people, it means bright clothes and a feast and for a few hours freedom from work and worry. It is very important for a bride and groom to have the best of luck and to have the gods smile on them, so the wedding festivities last for many days, if there is enough wealth to pay for the feast and the dancing and the bands. If the people are poor there is not so much of any of these things, but there is always a group of friends willing to stay by the couple until every bit of joy possible has been squeezed out of the event.

Westerners who have lived in India and who are sympathetic with Indian ways of religious thought are sometimes able to enter into the national feasts and festivals with the people. Even if they do not, they are made aware that something special is going on just by walking through the bazaar where they live. On the approach of a religious festival merchants stock up with extra wares for its observation. The usual color in the bazaar becomes gayer, the talk more excited, the movements more swift. Holiday feeling is in the air. The shops do a brisk business in clothing, colored sugar toys, supplies for making special kinds of food, and gifts.

In the home kitchens there is great preparation. The ritual of cooking and serving food is more strictly followed because it is festival time. If American children can imagine all the pleasures of our Christmas and Thanksgiving and Easter and Fourth of July happening every month or so, it will give them some idea of what goes on in India.

Each festival has some outward form, in addition to its being sacred to a particular god, which distinguishes it from every other. The reasons for each celebration are often lost in complicated mythology. But the old rites and rituals are followed as faithfully as they have been for many generations.

The loveliest of all the Hindu festivals, in the North at least, is Dasera time, which lasts ten days and is held in honor of the Rama legends. This holiday is especially dear to those Hindus who are descended from the warrior caste, because of Rama's brave exploits.

Dasera comes in October at the end of the long, wet, steamy months of the monsoon. The air clears after the rains, the gardens are fresh and green, and all the trees in leaf look washed and ready for the new season.

The women clean house. In the poorer homes new clay floors are patted down and smoothed by the skilled, patient hands of the housewives. In the homes of the well-to-do whitewashing is renewed on the walls and new rugs brought in. Those who can, buy new clothes. There is a great deal of food cooked. Some of it is offered in the temples and a part is sent to friends and there is always some set aside for the poor.

The children are not forgotten. Special sweets are made for them in the bazaar, sugar toys in the shape of animals tinted with delicate colors. Puffed rice is another great treat on this holiday.

Everyone plans to be with his family, if possible, at this time of year. Railroads run extra trains at excursion rates. Business firms plan to work only part time in their offices during Dasera. People date happenings as having taken place before or after this ten-day festival.

Diwali, the Feast of Lights, comes at the close of Dasera, on the tenth night. Then come the illuminations. For weeks all the potters have been working at their wheels day and night, turning out thousands of *chirags*, small, shallow red clay dishes, just large enough to hold a bit of oil, in which a twist of cotton wick may be floated. Most of the North India houses that are not thatched have flat roofs. The little lamps are set in rows around the roof edges and in window ledges of houses and public buildings, anywhere that a tiny light can be perched. If electricity can be had, as in large cities, strings of bulbs are used for the same purpose, but the oil lights are more beautiful.

On this tenth night the people expect that Lakshmi, the goddess who represents Mother Nature, will return from the hills where she has spent the long, hot summer, and bless the new season. Lakshmi corresponds to Ceres, goddess of the harvest, in the old Roman mythology. The Hindus who still cling to their ancient faith believe that the lights will guide the goddess on her way back to the plains, and if she sees well, the greater their blessing.

It is a great moment, as the darkness comes and the first small flame flickers uncertainly from one tiny lamp. Then its neighbor glows and the next and the next, until a line of light seems to run along the ledges and roofs everywhere. The crowds gathered in parks and on roof tops watch for that first flicker and a shout goes up. It seems to say that now the goddess will surely find her way.

Young girls light lamps of their own, making special wishes at the same time. They have a way of telling by the length of time each burns what their fortune will be. If they live near a river, the little lamp is set afloat on the water and if it burns until it has floated out of sight the girl knows she will have good luck until next Diwali.

Dasera and its final night, Diwali, are as close to the American way of celebrating Christmas and the New Year as any Hindu holiday can be, with a little of Thanksgiving thrown in. The thankfulness is for the end of the monsoon. Many pray for success in the coming year. Merchants begin new account books and ask the family priest to bless them in the name of Lakshmi.

Another festival connected with the seasons is the picturesque Teej in Jaipur State in Rajputana. This occurs in early April at the end of the spring harvest. On the third day—Teej means third—of a full week of celebration, the people go to Jaipur City to honor Gangur, the goddess of plenty. A great procession forms, led by richly dressed elephants, in which is carried the figure of the goddess. It is a gay crowd, with every color of the rainbow represented in the people's holiday dress. Teej is a time also when the people pay respect to their prince. He is the master of ceremonies. When the holiday is over the goddess is taken back to her shrine in the palace to wait for another harvest.

Tying the *rakhi*, the wrist thread, is a ceremony that was originally only religious. Later it became a social custom as well. This observance comes in the end of August all over upper India and it is one of the most significant of Hindu ceremonials. The rakhi used by the family priest is made of *mauli*, a red cotton yarn. He ties it around the wrist of each man who has prepared himself by following a prescribed act of worship. The priest then recites from Sanskrit ritual the charm, "I am tying this rakhi around your wrist so that you may be kept from harm and danger throughout the year." Each person so blessed gives a piece of money in return.

Socially this ceremony is more exciting, and the rakhi has become a much more elaborate twist of gold and silver thread with tassels, sometimes with jewels intertwined.

Sisters and girl cousins of the young men in a household dress in their best clothes, procure very beautiful wrist cords and go to their chosen relative to tie on the rakhi. The priest has no part in this aspect of the observance. The girls repeat the prayer for protection and offer sweets as they tie the cord. In return the girls receive gifts of money and each boy is bound by the wrist gift to protect his sister or cousin if she shall have need. In romantic stories about India the rakhi appears over and over again, in its social meaning, the man a prince, bound by it to protect a fair lady who is often not a relative.

In August, too, Krishna, the flute player, is honored on his birthday in the Hindu city of Brindaban where there are hundreds of temples. Fruit and flower decorations adorn the temples and there is much dancing and gaiety.

Krishna was a human prince but was supposed to be an earthly incarnation of Vishnu. On the evening before the birthday the people go to the temple to hear the story of his birth. A baby in a cradle, symbolizing the famous child, is shown at midnight and offerings of money and food are made at the shrine.

Tiny replicas of the feet of Krishna, made of pierced brass, are sold at this festival. They are used to make an imprint on the forehead of the worshipper, by first dipping in colored paste.

Cocoanut day in South India is their recognition of the end of the rainy season. People flock to the seashore and throw the shaggy nuts in as an offering to the gods of the sea winds. If the origin of this custom were traced, one would probably find that cocoanuts are chosen for offerings to the sea and to Shiva because, as abundant food supply, they represent life.

A festival of quite another sort is the great religious gathering, the Magh Mela, held in January every year at the junction of the Jumna River with the Ganges near the city of Allahabad in Uttar Pradesh. A *mela* is a religious fair. The people come in thousands to bathe in the sacred waters and to be cleansed of their sins. Special police have to be appointed to handle the crowd. Temporary shelters spring up in the low sandy flats between the river shores. Priests come and perform their daily ritual of worship. Holy men from all over India plan their wanderings to bring them to Allahabad at the appointed time.

A bazaar does good business at the Mela. Shopkeepers sell a lot of food. The people in attendance must live. Images of gods are there in all their best finery. The holy water of Mother Ganges is sold at the stalls in little sealed bottles to be taken home to distant villages.

The yellow clay dust kicked up by the crowds' feet hangs in the air like a stifling tent. At mid-day almost a summer warmth prevails because there are so many people. Water-men with full, dripping goatskins try to sprinkle the roadways. There is little laughter. In spite of the heat and the crowds the spirit of devotion rises to a high pitch.

Once in a while religious feast days are the source of much anxiety for the police and the government, if there should be a clash of two or more communities on that day. Such a clash happened several years ago and it was settled most ingeniously by a clever officer. The Hindus and the Muslims were the principals in the affair, which happened at Mohurram.

This is the annual mourning time for the death of two grandsons of the Prophet Mohammed. Elaborate preparations are made by the Muslims by building delicate reed or bamboo and tissue paper replicas of their tombs. These are called *tazias*. Sometimes small clay figures are placed inside. The paper tombs, some of which are very large and elaborately decorated, are carried in procession through the streets to a burial place outside the city or to some special place inside.

On this particular occasion, in a village near Lucknow the procession got as far on its way as a large pipal tree, where it was stopped. One of the frail tombs was too high to go under the tree which spread its shade out over the road. The Hindus refused to allow the offending tree limb to be cut off. The Muslims refused to go to their burial place by another route. They also refused to lower the tall tazia which was causing the trouble. The police were distracted. Then one of them had a good idea. Tools were sent for and the roadway was dug out beneath the tree limb. The procession could then pass and the tazia was not spoiled. The tree was not harmed, there was no riot, and everybody was happy.

There are many fairs which have no religious connection at all. They occur annually in different localities and are the occasion for bringing together in one place all the handcrafts and manufactures of a district. They last sometimes a whole week. A small city of shops springs up on an open space where cows and goats graze the rest of the year. A large tent is pitched for the headquarters of the town officials. A small formal garden appears in front of it overnight, with red brick-dust walks and grass plots edged by potted plants. There, on the first day a small afternoon durbar or reception is held and the Commissioner or the Chairman of the Municipal Board declares the *numaish*, the fair, open.

The shops are set in streets like those in a regular bazaar. All leather goods are in one place. All tin things are grouped in another. Toys are piled high in a third. Restaurants and tea stalls are on the outskirts. There is much bargaining. Prices are supposed to be better at the fair than at any other time during the year and many people wait until then to make important purchases.

The man selling glass bracelets does a roaring trade.

They are made in lovely colors, light and dark, and are the joy of schoolgirls and others who cannot afford silver and gold ones.

Though these fairs are organized for business there is a friendly spirit everywhere. Much money changes hands. A great deal of visiting goes on over a plate of curry and a cup of tea. The shops stay open in the evenings. Little girls ride around happily on their fathers' shoulders. Boys hang about, hoping to earn a few coins by carrying people's parcels for them. There is a "fair" smell hovering above the streets and flimsy small buildings. It is a grand mixture of the odors of sweets cooking in hot fat, of onions frying, of new leather and kerosene oil, mingled with those of freshly sprinkled roadways and the smoke from the merchants' pipes.

A fair is India in one of its best moods where the whole family may have pleasure together for only a small expenditure.

V. THE INDIAN WAY OF LIFE

WHILE it is true that any race or nation has special ways and customs which distinguish it from all the rest of the world, this has been perhaps more true of India than any other country.

Many customs in Indian life have developed from the needs and occupations of the people in ancient times and have never been changed. But more of them have been prescribed by Hindu law. It is these which have set India apart from other nations. Nowhere else in the world do we find the people divided into classes by rigid social rules which have their origin in the growth of a religion.

There is one thing common to all castes, however. Within each one the family is the center of all activity. They are a group closely bound together whose interests are the same.

Changing circumstances in government, in ways of making a living and easier travel have had an effect on the Indian social system. There are signs everywhere that caste barriers are breaking down. They are already less rigid than they have been for centuries. "The old order changeth, giving place unto new" is being demonstrated every day in modern India, but the love of home and loyalty to the family will always abide. The family is the very heart of Indian living.

14

THE WOMEN'S PART

THE WORK of looking after a house in India is much harder than it is in America. The mother of a family has to send the father off to his work in the morning. She, or another woman in the family, prepares breakfast and looks after the children. She keeps busy at something all day long. All these things the American mother does, but not at all in the same ways.

Housework in a country village in India is hardest of all. They do not have ice, so the food cannot be prepared very far ahead or in quantity, to save work, because it will spoil. Bread will last a day but by evening it becomes dry and hard.

Every drop of water used in the household must be

carried in. If it is a caste family the water is brought from the village well. If the family is low caste, or untouchable, sometimes the water has to be brought from a pond or from the river even farther away. The mother does this work unless there are children in the family old enough to help, who can be spared from other duties. Each member of a country family works at something.

Most of the cooking vessels are made of brass and these must be scoured clean after each using and made bright and shining again. This means polishing with the soft grey ash taken from the small *chula*, a low mud stove.

The mother and one of the little girls have even had a hand in making that ash. They start at the beginning of things in India. The beginning of fuel is the droppings of the cows. The children follow the cattle and collect it in a broad, shallow basket. At home they mix it with a little straw and pat it into cakes which are spread on the sides of the mud houses to dry. This is their fuel for cooking. Wood to burn is scarce and expensive and charcoal is a luxury that some village people never see.

The odor of the smoke from cooking fires is not unpleasant and the flame has a pretty color from the chemicals in the animals' bodies. However, an attempt is being made to put rural India back on a wood-burning basis so that these chemical properties can go back into the soil and thus help to produce more nourishing crops.

A walk across country fields at evening time in the early cold weather is a pleasant thing, with the smoke from those fires rolling low on the ground and mingling with the twilight mists. One hears the voices of the children calling to the cattle and the mothers calling to the children. A cowherd may be playing his pipe and a lone farmer, walking home with his plough on his shoulders, may be singing a pastorale for blessing on his crops or a tune to keep the evil spirits away. It will be a simple song, one measure repeated again and again, but it comforts the singer and cheers those who listen. Evening time is homecoming time in India as well as in America.

And then there is sleeping time when the food has been eaten, the last cow put in the byre for the night and the day's work done. The villagers have no light in their houses but firelight. The coals of fuel that are left in the cooking place must be carefully banked with the grey ash so that there will be a spark to kindle the breakfast flame in the morning. The door is shut and the family goes to sleep. They share the few warm quilts they have, if it is cold weather. In the hot season they sleep out in the open in the tiny *angan*, or courtyard, before the house, occupied possibly by their cow also.

Part of the mother's duty in the house is to look

after the shrine of the family god. The men may go to the temples to worship and make offerings to the god of the village and to ask for special blessing on the crops or a business deal. The women and children go to the temple less often, perhaps only on special feast days or ceremonial days. For them there is the shrine at home.

Each family has its own special god. It may be any one of a great number. It is probably one that the family has worshipped for many generations and the reason for adopting it as their own guardian has been forgotten, unless the story is handed down by mouth along with the religious legends and tales of ancient heroes. Usually the family shrine is a small niche in the mud wall of the house, hollowed out above the cooking place and there the little god figure sits and guards the household.

The prescribed way for morning worship to take place in a Hindu household is the old custom of making the five-fold offering, fresh every day, in a special set of shrine bowls not used for any other purpose. Each part of the offering is a symbol of the elements which make up life: water, food, a flower, fire and incense. A live coal is easily lifted from the hearth with a tongs; water is there in an earthen jar, brought in from the well; if not a flower, a fresh green leaf can surely be had from a nearby bush or plant; but the food is sometimes a problem. Even a few grains of rice, when cooked, are a mouthful for a member of the family.

So every one of the five bowls may not be filled but the purpose never changes and the faith of the family in the protection of their gods is strong.

In the early morning while the rest of the family is still asleep, the mother arises and blows life into the dull red coals hidden in the ashes of her fire. She performs her own private act of worship, cleansing her body, for the hearth is a sacred place and the one who cooks and serves the food must be worthy. Then she attends to the shrine for the day. There may be time, and enough powdered rice, to make a symbolic pattern before the doorway, as a sign of worship and reverence for the spirits who guard it. But there may not be a moment in a farmer's home in a village, because by this time the others are waking, and there is a long day's work ahead.

Far off a cock crows. A village dog barks. The smoke of the morning fire begins to curl up from the crackling dung cakes. The mother has washed her hands again by pouring water on them, dipped from the earthen jar. She is ready to roll out the chapatties, the unleavened bread of India. Sitting on the floor in front of the stove, she gathers round her the various things she will need.

There is the pan of dough, kneaded the night before, covered and set by the fire to wait until morning. The dough has been made from flour she herself has ground between two stones moving like a pair of wheels, laid flat one on top of the other. The flour runs down through a little groove. There is the tiny pastry board, a little larger than a large American pancake. The board is made of smooth wood and stands on three knobs which raise it off the floor a little. There is the small rolling pin. There is the metal dome on which the bread will bake. There is her *cheemta*, a band of metal bent double in the middle, like a long pincer, for handling the hot bread.

The cook tears off small amounts of the dough, each one big enough to make one piece of bread. She rolls this into a ball, between her two palms, then she flattens it in the same way and lays it on the pastry board to roll out thinner with the rolling pin. When it is the size of a pancake, the round of dough is laid on the metal dome above the glowing coals and cooked through on both sides. With the tongs it is lifted from the dome to the ashes, and allowed to steam there, puffing out into a big ball before it flattens again and is tossed into waiting hungry hands or into a basket where it is kept covered until all the family is ready to eat, though the father is served first of all.

The hot bread is a wonderful finger-warmer on a cold morning, and it has a lovely smell, like fresh whole-wheat bread from an American bakery, though it is not a yeast bread. It is torn apart in small pieces, to be eaten.

Enough bread is made in the morning so that the father may carry some with him to the field, or for a child to carry to him at mid-day. After he has gone to his work the mother feeds the baby and the other children.

Then the oldest girl takes the cows out to the grasslands alongside the road or the canal bank if they live near one. The girl may knit as she walks along, or she may carry the baby and tend it for her mother. The younger children have the basket for the droppings, and there may be some goats to look after.

When all is tidy in the little one-room mud house, the mother may have time to do a little spinning, though the process of making cloth from homespun thread is very slow. If she does not spin, the mother may join her husband in the field, working by his side until the sun tells her that the day is almost gone and she must hurry home to prepare the evening meal. They may have rice for that, or a tasty mixture of vegetables cooked together, or a gravy made of dried *dal* (a vegetable like peas) cooked until it is thick and mushy.

This is the way that rural India, the farming people, live.

Not all of the mothers of India live in country villages. Some live in large towns and their homes are in the bazaar, behind or above the husband's shop. If they are Muslim or high-caste Hindus they may never leave their homes except when, with faces covered, they occasionally pay visits to their own former homes. They depend for news upon the serving women who shop daily for food and bring in all the street corner gossip they can gather up. The lives of these women are full of simple home interests, their clothing and their children and a little visiting back and forth across roof tops with neighbor women like themselves.

Other mothers are educated women, who have defied ancient custom or have come from families who believe in progress and have taken up a professional career. There are women lawyers in India, and doctors and teachers and scientists. They have families and they run their households and carry on their professional life charmingly.

These women have done a great deal, in the All India Woman's Congress, to change existing laws for the betterment of all women, North and South. Their influence, working steadily year by year since 1926 when the organization was begun, has counted more than is realized in bringing about a united country. They have stood from the beginning for equality among women, no matter what the religious faith of each, or her caste, might be.

Palace housekeeping has its problems, too. The princes of India have town houses and country homes and are always entertaining guests. Some of these are Europeans who are put up in guest houses on the estate. The whole system at times resembles the organization of a private hotel and the staff of people necessary to keep it working smoothly is enormous.

European housewives make many funny mistakes in their Indian housekeeping if they have not troubled to learn the language of the part of the country in which their husbands are at work. They then have to depend on a house staff which is supposed to know English. Indian serving men are gentlemen. They never laugh when the mistress says an impossible thing. They have their fun later, out behind the cook house. Kitchens for European bungalows are usually arranged in a separate small building away from the house, as they used to be in plantations in the American South. There is give and take on both sides because Indian servants sometimes make funny errors in English. There was one household which never again called cake icing by any other name but "plaster" after the day that the cook solemnly indicated the sugar he was taking to make a cake and said that one cup of it was for the "plaster." The same cook made a platterful of sugar cookies the day the mistress had asked for baking powder biscuits. She should have said "scones" and all would have been well. The cookies were good, though there was a great *tamasha* before each understood the other.

Tamasha is a lovely word. It can be used for many things. Its basic, literal meaning is "something going on," or a "doings" as we say in our provincial speech in this country. It can mean a wedding or a fight or a program given by a juggler. It can mean a great emotional scene put on by a bad-tempered person. Let the word be merely whispered and a crowd gathers.

The mothers and homemakers of India and the women doctors and lawyers and university professors must be able to handle all tamashas and keep cheerful, even if it is something annoying. Women are proving that they can handle big tamashas in this new day of the Union of India. A woman was governor of a province until her death. That was Madame Sarojini Naidu, one of India's great poets, and an ardent nationalist. A woman is president of a college. That is Miss Sarah Chakko of Isabella Thoburn College in Lucknow. A woman has been in the Indian Cabinet as Minister for Health. That is Rajkumari Amrit Kaur. A woman was Ambassador to Washington until her resignation last year. That was Madame Vijayalakshmi Pandit.

When all the women of India learn the power they hold in their right to vote the elections will be good, stirring tamashas, too. But first some of them must learn to write their names. Others must learn public speaking and how politicians win elections. It will be an exciting life for many Indian women in the next few years.

It has been a long time since that first break-through in Zogi-La Pass when the mothers set up camp and found food for their tired children. Their spirit has been on the march ever since. It has survived wars and disease and famines and not knowing how to read and write. It will still endure as it marches on.

15

THE CHILDREN'S PART

THE CHILDREN of India are not different from other children, all over the world. They like to play and they get into mischief easily. The children themselves are not different but the conditions into which they are born make their lives different from those of children in America.

It may be a bit startling to read that many of the children of India do not go to school; that some of them never have time to play, not any at all; that others beg in city streets for a living; that a few live in royal palaces, with motor cars of their own. But all of these things are true.

The conditions which surround a child when it is born and during its growing up are those of its family.

The part any child has in its family's way of life is governed by those conditions.

The small son of a Hindu Rajah may have plenty to eat and have a clean place to sleep, and may ride out daily in his motor car, but he may be lonely because he has no other child to play with at games.

The village child may have plenty of playmates right in his own family and yet none of them may take time to play because they must work to help with the family's support.

There are many children in the towns whose fathers are neither rich nor poor. They go to good government schools. They go with their families to the hills in the hot weather. Some of them are even sent to schools in the hills. Their part in their family's way of life is to learn how to support themselves, either in a business or profession when they are grown. Their part is obedience to the Hindu law of loyalty to the family. They have no responsibility for anything else until they are grown.

But ninety percent of the children of India live in the villages. Their fathers are farmers. Their way of life is the difficult one of constant work, little play, no school. There are some exceptions but that is the rule. They have a responsibility to the family as soon as they are able to work. There is something to be busy with all of the time, even if it is no more than attending the family baby while following a herd of cows sent out to graze.

The British government provided free popular education, hiring teachers and setting up small schools in the villages. These have been poorly attended a great deal of the time. The government reckoned without the people themselves and the caste system. Government maintained that even though a child was an untouchable he still had the right to attend school. But caste boys refused to recite when such children came to school, and the teachers could not change the situation. The result was that the low caste and untouchable children stayed at home.

There are a few small pleasures for the hard-working village child. There are the annual fairs at which they have a few pice to spend. A pice is a piece of copper money which equals about half an American penny. There are bright clay and wood toys to buy; there are the favorite sweets; there is the merry-go-round, or a ferris wheel turned by hand and sometimes a man comes with a dusty, clumsy dancing bear.

Even with such delights, village life is not exciting and the little Indian girl and her brothers born into such homes have had the same dreary outlook ahead that their parents had, unless something happened to make a difference.

The difference is often the chance to go into the large town of the district and attend an American school, if the family is Christian, sometimes even if it is not, and if a promising child can be spared from the family work. Often the younger ones are put in the town school. It assures them good food and care.

In most of these town schools the children stay for ten months of the year, living in dormitories. They are much better fed than at home, and they have free time to play.

Little girls draw crude, uneven squares on the hard clay of the dormitory yard with charcoal or chalk. For markers they use bright bits of broken glass bracelets, of red clay water jars or smooth pebbles. With this simple equipment they play hopscotch or tit-tat-toe and other similar games of local invention.

The boys play hockey. If they can't get a real stick they will search until they find a tree branch that has grown with a bend at the proper place and out of it they fashion a rude substitute, scraping it smooth with a bit of broken glass. Their puck can be anything, an old tin can, a piece of cast-off wood from a carpenter's shop, a stone. But how they play! Hockey is an extremely popular game in India, comparable to the place baseball holds in America.

The children take their turn with yard and kitchen and dormitory duties. The girls work in groups at baking the bread, turning out enough chapatties for the whole school. Saturday is the day for laundry and extra hockey matches and perhaps the performance of a play. Real appreciation and understanding of acting seems to be born in most Indian children, whatever their ancestry may be.

By the old Hindu law which still affects the social

thinking even of Christians, a child so privileged as to receive a free education continues to have a responsibility within the family. It is his part to qualify for a better job than his father's when the time comes, so that he may help with the education of the younger members of the family.

Whether in or out of school, the village children who will grow up in the new state of India are fortunate. Life for them will be much better than it has been for their parents and grandparents. More of them will have an opportunity to be educated. There will be more food for which they will have to work less hard. This will come about through better methods of cultivation. This better life will come only gradually to the more remote rural places, but it will come.

Yet in coming it will not remove the ancient law of family life in India, each member having responsibility for and sharing in the activities which maintain the home.

16

THE MEN'S PART

A MAN's daily occupation is inherited in India. He is born to it, succeeding his father and his grandfather and his great-grandfather in whatever daily work the family does to support all its members.

Caste has ordered that each worker shall do only one kind of thing. This has been true ever since Hindus were divided into classes and the place of each class in the social system was fixed, linked to the kind of work done by the people belonging in it.

If a man's father was a silversmith or a goldsmith or a merchant or a herdsman, then he also became one, and his children after him, down through the generations. There was no way by which anyone could better his social position and remain a Hindu.

The rise and growth of great commercial industries has been one of the surest means of breaking down caste barriers. Men who had formerly worked at many different caste occupations began flocking to the cities to take jobs in cotton or steel mills, and they found that their whole daily life was changed. Caste was disregarded by the foreman in the mill who had to get a certain job done by a set time. The workmen stayed because they were able to make a better living for their families than by working in the old way.

The demand upon India's resources in World War II was another cause of caste break-down. The Parsees with their ability to get along with all communities have been one of the distinguished forces in this equality movement in India. The Tata Iron and Steel Company is a good example of this.

This company was established in 1911 when Mr. Jamshedji N. Tata discovered a rich vein of iron ore in Central India and called in American, English and German technical experts to help him start a steel business. There were other investors besides the Tata family but they have been the policy-makers of the scheme.

The site of the furnaces, not far from Calcutta, was named Jamshedpur for Mr. Tata (The City of Jamshed, literally). It has been marvellously successful from the start. Now it recruits its own technicians from the school maintained in connection with the plant where young Indian men are taught chemistry, physics, the science of metals and management. These young men are Buddhists. They are Muslims. They are Hindu Brahmans or lower castes. That is secondary. First of all, they are Tata's employees, and they play games together after hours on plant teams. They eat together, severest test of all. The Tata companies have improved the rate of pay for Indian labor and the standard of housing. Jobs with Tata are considered high prizes, in spite of the risk involved of breaking caste.

It was chiefly the older generation of orthodox Hindus who clung so tenaciously to caste lines and who opposed Indian union, unless caste would be retained. In spite of the democratic ways which are coming to India through modernized labor conditions, caste cannot be ended automatically, even by government regulation. Any custom which has lasted as long as this social system, with its roots so deeply twisted in and about and through every part of Hindu life, will last longer than overnight, even when it has been condemned.

But these economic and industrial and social changes are all affecting the life of the Indian family. If the father's way of earning the living is changed, if he is obliged to move to a new town and to break some caste rules, it makes a difference to each person he supports.

Meantime the daily life of India goes on and the fathers, with their hands, are earning the living for their families in both old and new ways. Some of those hands are rough from digging in the soil and guiding a plough handle and taking care of oxen out in the country. In the town there are the factories. There are also the artisans, those patient men of India, who sit all day long making beautiful utensils and ornaments of many kinds, from all sorts of materials.

Not all the things they make are for sale to foreign countries. Indians who can afford such things are good customers. There are traditional ornaments in Indian households—somewhere, usually, is a replica of a tree, of silver or gold, as the one symbol of life most understood and revered throughout Hinduism. There are small images of the gods for the family shrines. There is exquisite jewelry to adorn the women of the household. There are all the bowls and trays and cups of gold and silver that a wealthy family has use for. And these things are handmade.

The temples are also good customers. The incense-burners and trays and bowls used at the shrines are the finest work available although it is a common belief among India's artisans that the gods will be angry if a thing is made perfectly, because only gods may be perfect, not human beings. So an Indian pattern is never symmetrically true, though this is one of the distinctions of handmade work, anywhere, as compared to machine precision.

In recent years, in addition to providing carved ivory, carved wood, lacquered wood, rich embroideries and silver work for their own use, a large business in enameled brassware has developed to satisfy the tourist trade and foreign markets. The design is first etched on and the parts to receive color are scooped out. Then the lacquer is applied by hand while hot, and allowed to dry and harden. Afterward the whole is polished and the design stands out as if painted there.

The *lis-mani* pattern, a four-petaled lily, is popular in work from Moradabad, a locality known all over the North for its beautiful brassware. Turquoise blue is much used and a gorgeous ruby red. There is a rich marigold shade, too, which glows like the flowers themselves with an apparent inner light, a little like Japanese cloisonné.

The old-fashioned, finely etched brass ornaments, candlesticks, boxes, vases and rose bowls have given place to rich color and good profits. Anyone who owns some etched brass candlesticks or an intricately designed bowl or vase or coffee tray should keep it. This kind of work has been part of an older day in Indian art and is dying out.

Many Indian towns have become famous for a particular craft. Jaipur is another brass center but its patterns and use of color are so distinctive that it is possible easily to tell the difference from Moradabadi work. Pink and purple and green and blue and red are all used together in bands around a vase or the flat part of a tray table. It is difficult to choose which of the two towns produces the best work.

In old Delhi tourists are always taken to the Ivory Palace. This is a shop where exquisite ivory pieces of all sorts may be ordered or purchased. The hard ivory best suited for carving comes from Africa. Indian elephants' tusks seem of a softer quality. This ivory is used for the inlay work in rosewood and sandalwood which is done so exquisitely in South India. There are references in Sanskrit records to the ivory guilds of ancient times, the "workers in teeth". The modern industry in ivory dates back to the beginnings of trade with Greece and Rome. Until then the work had been largely inlay in palace doors or in furniture. No matter what the form, such work takes good eyesight, great patience and skill, and the workman should have no feeling of urgency or pressure.

At the Ivory Palace they will show models of any sort of Indian vehicle, complete down to the small bullock cart-driver's whip, made of a thin shred of ivory. They have the three monkeys—the blind one, the deaf one and the dumb one. They show small models of the Taj Mahal, sets of chess men, and exquisite boxes of all sizes carved in patterns of flowers and animals and gods which stand out like cameo against the thin shell of the base. Some of the more intricate pieces, such as a whole tusk made into a lamp, take years to complete and the prices are gauged accordingly.

Plain blue pottery, principally vases and bowls, comes from Delhi, too. There is another sort, a classic blue design on a white ground, made in Gwalior State, a region renowned in Rajput history.

Lucknow has a silver bazaar, and the Lucknow pattern is distinguishable from that of any other place where silver is made because somewhere in the design will be a palm tree, an elephant, a cobra or a fish, especially the fish, the symbol of the ancient kings of Oudh. On tea sets made in the jungle pattern the cobra is the handle of the teapot with the inflated hood at the top making a place to rest one's thumb in pouring. There is a border of plump fish around the top and an elephant perches on the lid.

South India men make beautiful boxes and envelope openers and paper weights of a hard black metal inlaid with intricate silver design. There is also handbeaten flat silver. Its hallmark is an elephant at the end of each handle.

The grape leaf motif is used on screens, book-ends and tables carved from *shisham* wood at Saharanpur, close to the foot of the Himalayas in North India.

Textiles from India, in many hues and forms, have long been popular in American markets, even more so in recent years because of the increasing interest of designers in Eastern materials. The thin tissue scarfs of Benares, interwoven with spun gold, and exquisite brocades and gold-embroidered velvets have been made into hats and evening bags and shoes for American women. Indian women like such things, too. The saris made in Murshidabad, of pure silk in deep, rich colors, can usually be recognized because of their distinctive design, usually a large Indian bird.

Back of each piece of carved wood, each silver bowl, each brass vase, each shimmering length of gold tissue or bright silk, is the patient man, with the skilled, fine fingers, who made it. Appreciation of rich color and the knowledge of the use of precious metals and other fine material is born in him, from centuries of enduring tradition in his family.

Young Indian fathers are turning nowadays to western activities for the work of their hands. They are piloting airplanes for the new commercial lines. They are commentators on radio programs and managers of moving picture companies or actors in their plays. They are good fathers. The Indian family is still a sound unit of human organization.

The greatest gift a Hindu father may have is a son. He knows then that when he dies he will have some one to crack his skull, to allow his spirit to go free before his body is cremated. His joy in his son, however, begins at birth. They are closely associated the rest of their lives, unless the child is sent away to school. Many well-to-do families employ tutors and have their children taught at home, to keep the circle complete.

In the hands of the fathers of India, as they work and vote, lies the future of their families, and so does, in a larger way, the future of the nation.

VI. INDIA AMONG THE NATIONS

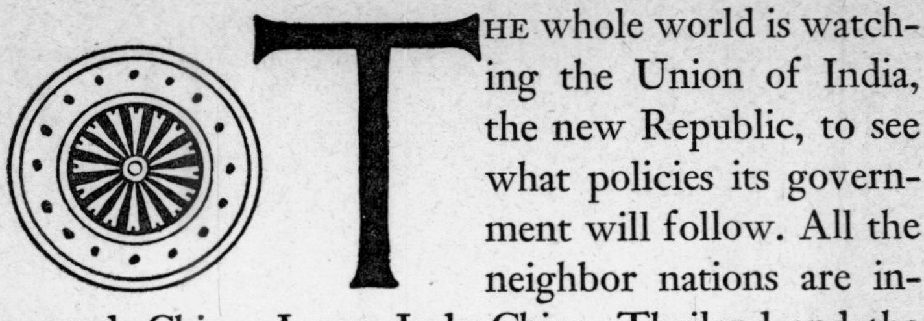

THE whole world is watching the Union of India, the new Republic, to see what policies its government will follow. All the neighbor nations are interested, China, Japan, Indo-China, Thailand and the rest. People of the West have a great concern.

Each period of the country's history has contributed something good as a guide to modern action. There was Asoka, the Buddhist, teaching peaceful relations with all men; there was Akbar, the tolerant Moghul; there were the strong, proud Rajputs. There was the commercial development of the early nineteenth century under the British East India Company. Participation in two World Wars, fighting as Imperial troops, has given India a superb Army. Her Navy is growing.

Present-day industrial development is rapid. There is great social change coming as the influence of caste on young people grows weaker.

India, the new nation, has already much power. If that power is used wisely, she has a great destiny.

17

THE NEW REPUBLIC, 1947–

MODERN INDIA, the new Republic, began its statehood on August 15, 1947, when, as representative of Great Britain, Lord Louis Mountbatten handed over the government of India to its own statesmen.

Following a short interim, the people voted in January, 1950, to become a Republic, in form of administration. A Constituent Assembly met in that month and on the twenty-second day they passed a Resolution to draw up a Constitution for the new state.

The Resolution contained some definite ideas to be embodied in that Constitution. One was that the power and authority of all the branches of government were to be derived from the people. Another was a guarantee of justice in social, economic, and political ways, to all the people; there was also to be equality for all individuals. Freedom of thought and worship were mentioned.

Those were bold and brave promises. They meant that caste would be done away with. It would have to be, if all men in India were to be considered equal. Legal holding of property was assured to men who had never been allowed to own any land. That meant land reforms. Freedom of thought and worship meant religious tolerance of each other by all the different groups of religious beliefs.

So the Republic was brought into being. Each generation, from the beginning of time, had handed on to the new state some quality of its own, some bit of learning. The sensible things in the ancient Code of Manu; the wisdom of Buddha, and the gentleness; the splendor and dignity of the Moghuls and the fiery bravery of the Rajputs; the dramatic ability of generations of poets and writers and dancers and the passion in Indian music; all these inspired the thoughts of the men who planned something big and brave and audacious for India.

The national flag is a horizontal tricolor of equal widths, saffron yellow on top, white in the middle and dark green in the lower stripe. In the middle of the white stripe is the wheel of Asoka. A flag raising ceremony was observed in the Red Fort at Delhi on August 16, 1947, and in an address on that occasion Prime Minister Nehru said, in part:

"When this flag was devised . . . we thought of a flag which would in its combination and in its separate parts somehow represent the spirit of the nation, the tradition of the nation . . . That wheel is a symbol of India's ancient culture, it is a symbol of the many things that India has stood for through the ages . . . It is well that our minds should go back towards India's ancient days. If India had not stood for something very great, I do not think that India could have survived and carried on its cultural traditions in a continuous manner through these vast ages."

There is another interpretation of the things the Indian flag stands for. The saffron stripe is the color of a Buddhist monk's robe, denoting devotion to spiritual values and forgetting material gain. The white stripe is the light of truth. The green stripe is the union of the products of the earth with man's mind. And the wheel means movement, a going forward and acceptance of change, for that is progress.

The design of the state seal is taken from the capital of the Lion Pillar of Sarnath, one of the Asoka pillars still in existence. The wheel appears there on the base of the capital between a bull and a horse and this section supports three lions, sitting back to back.

There is also a lotus on the Lion Pillar at Sarnath. Its partly opened petals seem to enfold and support the upper section where the animals are carved, separated by a wheel. If the entire capital had been used as the design for the state seal it would have been too long. So the lotus was omitted from the seal and instead was made the state flower.

The symbol of the wheel will mean many things in the coming years. Now it is the wheel of discipline, as well as of progress, rolling the new state into its place among the nations.

On January 24, 1950, a poem written by Rabindranath Tagore, *Jana Gana Mana*, was officially adopted as the Indian national anthem and music scores were later arranged for symphony, band and piano.

There will be new government medals to take the place of the old Empire honors, except the Star of India, which is being retained.

With this rich background and concept, the new Republic is reaching out to other nations with friendly hands. At present the government has diplomatic relations with twenty-four foreign powers.

It is customary in any new organization to take stock at the beginning, in somewhat the manner of a merchant taking inventory at the beginning of a new year. He sets down on one side everything he has on hand which is paid for and in good order. On the other side he writes down the things he still has to pay for in the coming months, his outstanding bills. What he has left is called the balance, with which he plans to operate his business.

At the outset the new Republic had one valuable asset, and that was the good will of the whole world, including Great Britain. It is not something that can be seen, or put on a shelf or in the bank. It is something that can be felt.

Then there are the rich material resources, things which may be seen. Although from North to South, India is predominantly an agricultural country, she has rich mines, gold and silver and iron and coal and many of the other treasures which this atomic age has made doubly important.

Among these is beryl. This is a milky-green stone, known to Indian princes for centuries, and the best quality is regarded by them to be almost as valuable as emeralds. World War II increased that value, for beryllium was found to be a powerful alloy. Used with copper it made a tougher metal. Bearings in fighting planes were made of this stone, providing greater safety. Even the children helped when the urgent need of beryl became known. They joined the searchers in the dry, gravelly hills of Rajputana and brought in the little green pebbles which eventually found their way to American ore mills.

Mica was another contribution to the needs of the war. Its use has been known in India for many years, but it was valued primarily for ornament in buildings and on clothing until electricity came into commoner use. Then radio and other electric equipment for which mica was needed immediately increased the value of mica mines. This material was flown to America in hundreds of tons.

India has also salt and cotton and valuable and beautiful hardwood which is used for ship and furniture building. She has manganese, used in making steel. She supplies goatskins for ladies' handbags and flyers' jackets and gloves. She has many new, growing industries, steel mills, motor car and airplane factories.

This partial list of India's resources proves that it is not a poor country. Under one government, with possible regulation of production and manufacture, everything can gradually be systematized for the common good. Out of Mother Earth, in a practical way, India will provide for her people.

The Indian Army has been well trained by its long service under the British. Indian troops have served well in many parts of the world. They were in Italy in World War II. They were at Dunkerque. Their regiments have a long and enviable service record.

India is fast developing a Navy. The first Indian home-built modern naval vessel, christened the *Jala Usha,* was launched at Vizagapalam in South India on March 14, 1948. It was a single screw cargo steamer of 8,000 tons and it was built entirely by Indian labor and financed by Indian capital. Vizagapalam has a fine harbor and suitable tidal range which allows ships to be launched at any season of the year. Now the yard has a capacity for producing two such ships as the *Jala Usha* in a year.

There are some things on the other side of the balance sheet which India must take care of before the new nation can be considered well established.

One is the completely unforeseen problem of finding homes and occupation for the many people who have been displaced by the recent civil war which followed partition. This is hurrying the growth of co-operative schemes as nothing else could have done. It is having a healthy influence on the breaking down of caste barriers, as people work together to build towns where none were before. The refugees will live in those towns and work in them.

Land reform will not be easy and it will be only a gradual process in spite of the brave words in the new Constitution.

The form of the new government had to be one which would give a fair share of participation to all the different groups of people in India. The one finally chosen is a Union of the Provinces formerly under the Viceroys and the Princely States. There is a president elected for a five-year term. Representation of the [illegible]tes and Provinces in the government is modeled somewhat on that of the United States.

Early in 1952 India had its first general election, as prescribed [illegible]e new constitution. It proved to be an enormo[illegible]vieldy operation. There were many unexpecte[illegible]gs which hindered the planned routine. Voting is a novelty and not understood. In one place a man was discovered on his knees worshipping the ballot box in the booth after he had voted. With experience future elections will go more smoothly.

Other hopes will be realized as well, by the slow turning of the Wheel of Progress upon which India's future is securely mounted. The wheel was one of the earliest and greatest discoveries of ancient man and in India its symbolism has guided the thoughts of people for centuries. Asoka's wheel has been turning toward this time for two thousand years and now it has made a full circle, back to the place where it began—tolerance and freedom of thought and peaceful relations with all men.

These are the principles which form the foundation of the Union of India, the new Republic among the nations.